Ancient CONTEXT
Ancient FAITH

ENCOUNTERS
WITH JESUS

UNCOVER THE ANCIENT CULTURE, DISCOVER HIDDEN MEANINGS

GARY M. BURGE

ZONDERVAN®

ZONDERVAN.com/
AUTHORTRACKER
follow your favorite authors

ZONDERVAN

Encounters with Jesus
Copyright © 2010 by Gary M. Burge

This title is also available as a Zondervan ebook.
Visit www.zondervan.com/ebooks.

Requests for information should be addressed to:

Zondervan, *Grand Rapids, Michigan 49530*

Library of Congress Cataloging-in-Publication Data

Burge, Gary M.
     Encounters with Jesus / Gary M. Burge.
        p. cm. (ancient context, ancient faith)
     Includes bibliographical references and index.
     ISBN 978-0-310-28046-0 (softcover)
     1. Jesus Christ — Friends and associates. I. Title.
  BT340.B87 2010
  232.9'5 — dc22
                                         2009040175

All Scripture quotations, unless otherwise indicated, are taken from the Holy Bible, *Today's New International Version®, TNIV®.* Copyright © 2001, 2005 by Biblica, Inc.™ Used by permission of Zondervan. All rights reserved worldwide.

Maps by International Mapping. Copyright © 2010 by Zondervan. All rights reserved.

Any Internet addresses (websites, blogs, etc.) and telephone numbers printed in this book are offered as a resource. They are not intended in any way to be or imply an endorsement by Zondervan, nor does Zondervan vouch for the content of these sites and numbers for the life of this book.

Cover and Interior design: Kirk DouPonce, www.DogEaredDesign.com
Cover photo: © Holmes Photography / CIR, Inc.

Printed in China

---

10 11 12 13 14 15 /CTC/ 23 22 21 20 19 18 17 16 15 14 13 12 11 10 9 8 7 6 5 4 3 2 1

For Matt and Ashleigh

CONTENTS

SERIES INTRODUCTION   7
Ancient Context, Ancient Faith

1   **ENCOUNTERING JESUS**   13

2   **THE WOMAN WITH THE HEMORRHAGE**   39
Matthew 9:18–26; Mark 5:21–43

3   **ZACCHAEUS OF JERICHO**   55
Luke 19:1–10

4   **THE CENTURION OF CAPERNAUM**   73
Luke 7:1–10

5   **A WOMAN IN SAMARIA**   95
John 4:4–26

6   **A GREEK WOMAN IN TYRE**   111
Matthew 15:21–28; Mark 7:24–30

ANCIENT CONTEXT, ANCIENT FAITH

EVERY COMMUNITY of Christians throughout history has framed its understanding of spiritual life within the context of its own culture. Byzantine Christians living in the fifth century and Puritan Christians living over a thousand years later used the world in which they lived to work out the principles of Christian faith, life, and identity. The reflex to build house churches, monastic communities, medieval cathedrals, steeple-graced and village-centered churches, or auditoriums with theater seating will always spring from the dominant cultural forces around us.

Even the way we understand "faith in Christ" is to some degree shaped by these cultural forces. For instance, in the last three hundred years, Western Christians have abandoned seeing faith as a chiefly communal exercise (although this is not true in Africa or Asia). Among the many endowments of the European Enlightenment, individualism reigns supreme: Christian faith is a personal, private endeavor. We prefer to say, *"I have accepted Christ,"* rather than define ourselves through a *community* that follows Christ. Likewise (again, thanks to the Enlightenment), we have elevated rationalism as a premier value. Among many Christians faith is a construct of the mind, an effort at knowledge gained through study, an assent to a set of theological propositions. Sometimes even knowing *what you believe* trumps belief itself.

To be sure, many Christians today are challenging these Enlightenment assumptions and are seeking to chart a new path. Nevertheless, this new path is as much a by-product of modern cultural trends than any other. For example, we live today in a highly therapeutic society. Even if we are unaware of the discipline of psychology, we are still being shaped by the values it has brought to our culture over the last hundred years. Faith today has an emotional, feeling-centered basis. Worship is measured by the emotive responses and the heart. "Felt needs" of a congregation shape many sermons.

Therefore, defining Christian faith as a personal choice based on well-informed convictions and inspired by emotionally engaging worship is a formula for spiritual formation that may be natural to us — but it may have elements that are foreign to the experience of other Christians in other cultures or other centuries. I imagine that fifth-century Christians would feel utterly lost in a modern church with its worship band and theater seating where lighting, sound, refreshments, and visual media are closely monitored. They might wonder if this *modern church* was chiefly indebted to entertainment, like a tamed, baptized version of Rome's public arenas. They might also wonder how ten thousand people can gain any sense of shared life or community when each family comes and goes by car, lives a long distance away, and barely recognizes the person sitting next to them.

THE ANCIENT LANDSCAPE

If it is true that *every* culture provides a framework in which the spiritual life is understood, the same must be said about the ancient world. The setting of Jesus and Paul in the Roman Empire was likewise shaped by cultural forces quite different from our own. If we fail to understand these cultural forces, we will fail to understand many of the things Jesus and Paul taught.

This does not mean that the culture of the biblical world enjoys some sort of divine approval or endorsement. We do not need to imitate the biblical world in order to live a more biblical life. This was a culture that had its own preferences for dress, speech, diet, music, intellectual thought, religious expression, and personal identity. And its cultural values were no more significant than are our own. Modesty in antiquity was expressed in a way we may not understand. The arrangement of marriage partners is foreign to our world of personal dating. Even how one prays (seated or standing, arms upraised or folded, aloud or silent) has norms dictated by culture.

But if this is true—if cultural values are presupposed within every faithful community, both now and two thousand years ago—then the stories we read in the Bible may presuppose themes that are completely obscure to us. Moreover, when we read the Bible, we may misrepresent its message because we simply do not understand the cultural instincts of the first century. We live two thousand years distant; we live in the West, and the ancient Middle East is not native territory for us.

INTERPRETING FROM AFAR

This means we must be cautious interpreters of the Bible. We must be careful lest we presuppose that *our cultural instincts* are the same as those represented in the Bible. We must be *culturally aware* of our own place in time—and we must work to comprehend the cultural context of the Scriptures that we wish to understand. Too often interpreters have lacked cultural awareness when reading the Scriptures. We have failed to recognize the gulf that exists between who we are today and the context of the Bible. We have forgotten that we read the Bible as foreigners, as visitors who have traveled not only to a new geography but a new century. We are literary tourists who are deeply in need of a guide.

The goal of this series is to be such a guide—to explore themes from the biblical world that are often misunderstood. In what sense, for instance, did the physical geography of Israel shape its people's sense of spirituality? How did the storytelling of Jesus presuppose cultural themes now lost to us? What celebrations did Jesus know intimately (such as a child's birth, a wedding, or a burial)? What agricultural or religious festivals did he attend? How did he use common images of labor or village life or social hierarchy when he taught? Did he use humor or allude to politics? In many cases — just as in our world — the more delicate matters are handled indirectly, and it takes expert guidance to revisit their correct meaning.

In short, this series employs *cultural anthropology, archaeology,* and *contextual backgrounds* to open up new vistas for the Christian reader. If the average reader suddenly sees a story or an idea in a new way, if a familiar passage is suddenly opened for new meaning and application, this effort has succeeded.

I am indebted to many experiences and people who awakened my sense of urgency about this interpretive method. My first encounter came as a student at Beirut's Near East School of Theology in the 1970s. Since then, scholars such as David Daube, J. D. M. Derrett, S. Safrai, M. Stern, E. P. Sanders, Charles Kraft, James Strange, Kenneth Bailey, Bruce Malina, I. Howard Marshall, and a host of others have contributed to how I read the New Testament. Bailey's many books in particular as well as his long friendship have been prominent in inspiring my efforts into the cultural anthropology of the ancient world. In addition, I have been welcomed many times by the Arabic-speaking church in Lebanon, Syria, Iraq, Jordan, Palestine, and Egypt and there became attuned to the way that cultural setting influences how we read texts. To them and their great and historic faith, I owe a considerable debt.

Finally, special thanks are due to Katya Coverett and Verlyn Vebrugge at Zondervan Publishing. Verlyn's expert editing and Katya's creativity improved the book enormously. In addition, Kim Tanner at Zondervan worked as senior visual content editor. Her skill at finding the unusual, arresting photo within huge archives never ceases to amaze me.

Soli Deo Gloria.

Gary M. Burge
Wheaton, Illinois

Chapter 1

ENCOUNTERING JESUS

HAVE YOU ever wondered what it would be like to encounter Jesus personally? We often fill this scene with our own imagined ideas of what he was like and how he connected to people. Compassion, strength, patience, wisdom, gentleness—these are some of the values we project onto him. And many are accurate. But I wonder if such scenes need to be shaped instead by real stories we have in the Gospels.

One of the more surprising features of Jesus' ministry was his willingness to have personal encounters with people. In some cases they were keenly interested in him and wanted to explore how they might become his followers. Occasionally they were well-placed leaders, tax collectors or military officials perhaps, and Jesus moved directly into their personal worlds. In other cases, Jesus met people with profound, debilitating health needs, and he stopped to see what could be done. Even children were quickly and easily drawn to him, and stories remain that describe how he reacted.

Records of famous teachers from the ancient world rarely offer us such accounts. Rare is the leader who was known for his engagement with the needy. Rarer still is the detailed

THE GALILEE VILLAGE OF GAMLA, DESTROYED BY THE ROMANS DURING THE WAR OF AD 66-70.

Z. Radovan/www.BibleLandPictures.com

A SILVER DENARIUS DEPICTING THE ROMAN MILITARY.

narrative of the rabbi or sage who invested in the personal troubles of the poor. But this must have been a hallmark of Jesus' presence in Galilee. He did not organize a school in a well-known city such as Jerusalem and invite people to come for lectures. Nor did he anchor himself in a remote location and permit seekers to find their way into the desert or mountains. Near the Dead Sea a first-century community we call Qumran built such a remote place, and its "Teacher of Righteousness" (as the Qumran Dead Sea Scrolls refer to him) lived there and taught hundreds of disciples. In the medieval era, Jewish mystics located themselves in a village called Safed

JESUS WAS KNOWN FOR SPENDING TIME WITH THOSE LESS FORTUNATE, LIKE WOMEN, CHILDREN, AND THE POOR. THIS IS CLEARLY PORTRAYED IN THE PAINTING *JESUS AND THE CHILDREN* BY LUCAS CRANACH (1472–1553).

ENCOUNTERS WITH JESUS

THE DESERT COMMUNITY OF QUMRAN, LOCATION OF THE DEAD SEA SCROLLS.

and in the remoteness of Galilee's northern mountains invited Jewish inquirers to join them.

Jesus did none of these things. After his tumultuous departure from Nazareth (Luke 4:16–30), Jesus moved to Capernaum on the north shore of the Sea of Galilee (Luke 4:31) and there

AERIAL VIEW OF MODERN SAFED, LOCATED IN UPPER GALILEE.

CHAPTER ONE, ENCOUNTERING JESUS

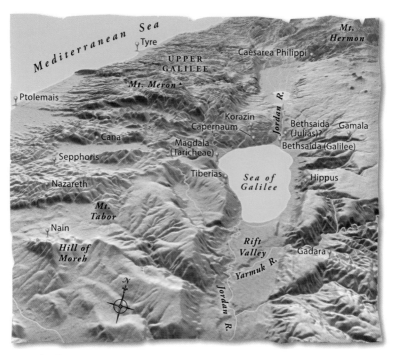

| CAPERNAUM AND SURROUNDING AREA

made his new home (Mark 2:1). This did attract many people, who sought him out, to the Capernaum synagogue but this village never became his *platform* for ministry per se. On one occasion while he was in the village, word got out that he was home, and suddenly Jesus found himself stuck in a small village house, overrun by eager, needy people (Mark 2:1–12). But most of his efforts happened elsewhere. It was near here that Jesus met the crowd of five thousand who were so riveted by his teaching and would not move despite their hunger—which Jesus resolved with a miracle (Mark 6:30–45). We know this took place on a hill not far from Capernaum since afterward a debate broke out in the Capernaum synagogue near the shore (John 6:59).

But this was not the usual state of affairs for Jesus and his entourage of twelve. Jesus moved around the country, visiting the many villages that dotted the landscape. Implicit in his call to the apostles was the notion that a part of the costliness of being his follower was that their location would change. Men who had been fishing all their lives—men whose homes were in Bethsaida or Capernaum—suddenly learned that Jesus was going to be on the road reaching people who had not come looking for him. Jesus hinted at this when he referred to foxes having holes to live in and birds having nests, but he would have nothing similar (Matt. 8:20). On occasion these followers were happy with the plan. At other times they were exasperated, such as when Peter complained, "We have left everything to follow you!" (Matt. 19:27). And at times they were impatient with the inefficiencies of Jesus' willingness to pause and be interrupted by the slightest need.

The great record of Jesus' life found in the Gospels is not merely a catalogue of his teachings, although this is important. Nor is it only an account of his great works. What is unique about the Gospels are the unexpected stories that detail Jesus' regular interruptions. *Jesus took time for people who generally assumed that they were invisible.* And what remains from those interruptions are stories that show the remarkable extent to which Jesus affected individual lives.

In other words, the "great canvas" on which the story of Christ was painted is not simply filled with large crowds, theological debates, Herodian intrigue, and Roman power. The gospel writers left surprising room for the individual story, the personal account, the transformed person. The measure of this messianic task was not found simply in its numbers or in its "successes," however that may be measured. The Gospels

THE EXCAVATED VILLAGE PATH AND FIRST-CENTURY HOMES OF THE GALILEE VILLAGE OF BETHSAIDA.

are filled with unexpected humble victories, quiet stories of children and lepers and the hopeless, who rarely appear on anyone's agenda. Sometimes these are major leaders of some importance who have private contact with him — but their appearance in the story has less to do with their stature or money or position than it does with their approach to Jesus and their willingness to be encountered.

JESUS AND THE POOR

Scholars agree that of all the Old Testament prophecies that were critical to Jesus' sense of mission, Isaiah 61 stands out.

> *The Spirit of the Sovereign LORD is on me,*
> > *because the LORD has anointed me*
> > *to proclaim good news to the poor.*
> *He has sent me to bind up the brokenhearted,*
> > *to proclaim freedom for the captives*
> > *and release from darkness for the prisoners. . . (Isa. 61:1)*

Jesus quoted this passage in the Nazareth synagogue when its leaders invited him to read aloud (Luke 4:16 – 21). And when the imprisoned John the Baptist felt dismayed, this was the citation Jesus sent back (Matt. 11:5). Isaiah 61 may even rest behind the Sermon on the Mount. Isaiah spoke of preaching good news to the poor — Jesus spoke of blessing the poor (Matt. 5:3). We

THE ROMAN FORTRESS OF MACHAERUS WHERE (ACCORDING TO JOSEPHUS) JOHN THE BAPTIST WAS IMPRISONED AND DIED.

wouldn't be far wrong to think about Isaiah 61 as the one biblical passage through which Jesus defined himself and his work.

Interest in the poor shouldn't surprise us since Jesus was familiar with poverty. He was raised in a small Galilee village that was so insignificant that it wasn't mentioned in the Old Testament or any rabbinic literature. Nathanael's ques-

JESUS' FATHER, JOSEPH, AS A CARPENTER IN A PAINTING BY GEORGES DE LA TOUR (1593–1652).

tion, "Nazareth! Can anything good come from there?" (John 1:46) probably reflects a well-known sentiment. Nazareth was not a prestigious village. Jesus' father was also a "builder" (Gk. *tekton*), not a landowner, and this placed the family among the lower socioeconomic classes.

When Jesus taught, "Blessed are the meek, for they will inherit the [land]" (Matt. 5:5), he may well have had the landless poor in mind. This is true for another blessing: "Blessed are you who hunger now, for you will be satisfied" (Luke 6:21). Even his parables reflect his understanding of the anxieties of the poor (Matt. 6:25–33) and their concern about debt. The Lord's

A POTTERY PAINTING DEPICTING A SLAVE GIRL IN THE HELLENISTIC PERIOD.

TWO SMALL COINS (GREEK: *LEPTA*) OFTEN
IDENTIFIED AS THE MONEY DEPOSITED BY THE
WIDOW IN MARK 12:31–44.

Prayer sums up their worries concisely: "Give us today our daily bread. And forgive us our debts . . ." (Matt. 6:11–12).

From this profile it doesn't surprise us that the Gospels have preserved stories about Jesus encountering people on both sides of the economic spectrum. In Mark 10, Jesus is approached by a rich man, and typically he pauses to listen to his story. And when the man expresses his worry about entering heaven, Jesus responds, "Go, sell everything you have and give to the poor, and you will have treasure in heaven. Then come, follow me" (Mark 10:21).

A PEARL AND
GOLD EARRING
FROM THE
ROMAN
EMPIRE.

On another occasion Jesus was in the temple watching people deposit their offerings. There he noticed a poor widow who put in two small copper coins. He remarked, "Truly I tell you, this poor widow has put more into the treasury than all the others. They all gave out of their wealth; but she, out of her poverty, put in everything" (Mark 12:43–44).

Even his followers were alert to the poor. When Jesus was anointed in Bethany with costly perfume, some of his followers complained that this could have been sold and distributed to the poor (Mark 14:5).

All of this reminds us that Jesus was remarkably attentive to the financial or material needs of those around him. His approach does not hint at a class struggle that discriminated against the rich. He certainly warned them about the risks of wealth (Matt. 19:24). But he did not simply pontificate about money. He noticed people. He noticed the poor. And as an influential teacher with growing fame, he was never above being with those of humble means.

JESUS AND THE SICK

Illnesses in many forms were common throughout Jesus' world. It is easy to forget how tenuous life was during the first century. This was a world without antibiotics, where surgery was "experimental," and medicine owed as much to magic than anything else. Injuries that we take for granted—such as wounds from farming implements—might easily lead to life-threatening infections. Today we would have to travel to rural areas of the developing world to see similar conditions.

As in many poverty-prone areas of the world today, infections of the eye were common. I am sometimes astonished at how often I have seen this in places like rural Egypt. Africa

SURGICAL INSTRUMENTS FROM ROMAN JUDEA.

Z. Radovan/www.BibleLandPictures.com

VOTIVE OFFERING, GIVEN TO ASCLEPIUS, THE GREEK GOD OF HEALING, WERE MODELS OF THE BODY PART THAT HAD BEEN HEALED. HERE IN A FIFTH-CENTURY MARBLE RELIEF (FROM EPIDAUROS, GREECE) A MAN PRESENTS A MODEL OF HIS LEG AS AN OFFERING TO ASCLEPIUS IN THANKS FOR HEALING HIS VARICOSE VEINS. TEMPLES TO ASCLEPIUS COLLECTED THOUSANDS OF SUCH OFFERINGS.

and the Amazon basin have similar problems. One of the few accounts of a medicinal treatment of the eyes comes from a Jewish book called Tobit, a novel written about a hundred years before Jesus. Tobit was a man who traveled to Nineveh (in modern-day Iraq) to see his father. However, his father was blind, with a white opaque film over his corneas. Tobit applied fish gall (or bile) to his eyes, which burned them—and when his father rubbed his eyes vigorously, the white film over them apparently peeled off and he could see (Tobit 11). Welcome to the world of ancient medicine.

But the same could be said for common injuries. The broken limb could lead to a life-crippling condition. A respiratory illness could cause death. Public sanitation was primitive, and diseases related to hygiene were well-known. Simply exploring the bathing practices of the ancient world gives some indication of their situation. Soap was relatively uncommon. Records indicate that even though the ancient Babylonians and Egyptians experimented with substances that enhanced washing, still, their detergent properties (using animal tallow and ash, or oils such as olive and lye) were often unsuccessful. It wasn't until the late Roman era that using a detergent for the body became common among the wealthy.

But in Jesus' day, bathing was often done with scented olive oil that was scraped from the skin with a tool called a *strigil*.

Wealthy Romans visited public baths, where a series of cold (*frigidarium*), warm (*tepedarium*), and hot baths (*caldarium*) were used in sequence to promote sweating as slaves scrapped oiled skin or used sponges. Today a brilliant, well-preserved example of these baths can be seen at the archaeological site of Scythopolis in the Jezreel Valley just south of Galilee.

Among the poor, hygiene as we know it today, with its disease-preventing properties, was unknown. This may well explain the many instances of sickness recorded throughout antiquity.

POTTERY SHOWING AN ATHLETE WITH STRIGIL HANGING NEARBY.

www.HolyLandPhotos.org

STRIGIL USED IN THE ROMAN ERA FOR CLEANSING THE SKIN.

www.HolyLandPhotos.org

PUBLIC TOILETS TYPICAL OF THOSE FOUND THROUGHOUT THE ROMAN EMPIRE.

© William D. Mounce

THE HEATED BATHHOUSE (OR CAULDARIUM) AT ROMAN SCYTHOPOLIS (OLD TESTAMENT BETH SHEAN).

Because there was no direct causal link to microscopic germs, people often turned to spiritual forces or demons to explain phenomena. While there is no doubt that the Gospels present a world with real demons troubling real people, still, this may also be the language for sickness. The Gospels record four long stories of exorcisms (Mark 1:21–28; 5:1–20; 7:24–30; 9:14–29), a short report of an exorcism (Matt. 9:32–34; cf.

A SIXTH-CENTURY MOSAIC SHOWING CHRIST PERFORMING AN EXORCISM.

THE DECAPOLIS CITY OF GADARA, LIKELY
HOME OF THE DEMONIAC IN MATTHEW 8.

12:22), and general references to this as one of Jesus' works
(Mark 1:32–34). In some cases, a deaf person was said to have a
"spirit" of deafness (Mark 9:25). In Mark 9:14–29 the boy who
is healed may have had epilepsy.

Yet the Gadarene demoniac (Mark 5) defies health catego-
ries (is this mental illness?) and explic-
itly points to demonic oppression. Evil spirits and sickness were seen in close connection (see Luke 8:2).

The Gospels are eager to report that Jesus contacted people with any known illness. He exhibits no fear of acquiring the sickness himself. While Old Testament law, Jewish custom, Hippocrates, and even the advice of Roman physicians such

THE USE OF MAGIC WAS COMMON
IN JESUS' TIME. INCANTATION
BOWLS WERE PLACED WITH THE
BOTTOM UP UNDER THE FLOORS
AND THRESHOLDS OF HOUSES.
THE DEMONS WERE THEN
BELIEVED TO BE TRAPPED INSIDE
THE BOWL, WITH THE MAGICAL
SPELLS WRITTEN AGAINST THEM.

as Galen called for the exclusion or isolation of those who were ill, Jesus not only heals them but touches them. This is underscored when we read about lepers and a woman with a "flow of blood." These stories bear more meaning than we might at first think. Further, no conflict with any demon ever suggests that Jesus is in jeopardy. He uses no magical formulae, no potent saying, and no sacred implements fill his repertoire. He simply commands them and they are defeated.

JESUS AND THE POWERFUL

The social and political landscape of first-century Judea also included the powerful. These were persons who were well-placed financially, who facilitated the Roman occupation, or who were in the administrative bureaucracy of the province. A casual reference in Luke 8:3 hints that Jesus had genuine access to these people. Here Luke lists the women following Jesus, among whom he mentions Joanna, the wife of Chuza, Herod's steward. We cannot be sure if this note implies that she was wealthy or had high status; we do not even know if she left her husband and was a follower (a secret follower?) of Jesus. But we do know that she was married to someone who had power in Galilee's ruling elite.

Luke continues by referring to another woman who fol-

AN EXQUISITE MOSAIC IN A VILLA IN ANCIENT SEPPHORIS OF GALILEE. OFTEN CALLED 'THE MONA LISA OF GALILEE.'

lowed Jesus: "Susanna, and many others . . . [who] were helping to support them out of their own means." These scant
verses suggest that there were influential and powerful people
who were willing to be encountered by Jesus and even support
him financially.

Jesus' world was stratified like so much of the Roman
empire. There were leaders who occupied significant positions
with the imperial rulers, and there were others who maintained the systems that brought in taxation and sustained the
military occupation. Scholars often speak of four "strata" that

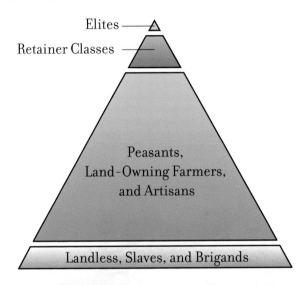

likely made up Judean society in Jesus' day. In many presenta-
tions, they form a pyramid.

(1) At the narrow top there were the "elites," who were the
ruling aristocracy. This might be Herod Antipas or members
of the Herodian dynasty, who could be found in Jerusalem,
Sepphoris, or Tiberius. They lived in luxury but were always
subject to the whims of the Roman empire and its interests.
Some might include the high priest in this category.

(2) The next class is what we could call the "retainer" classes.
These were people who were middle managers, who implemented the world of control and taxation. They were estate
managers, prison guards, tax collectors, the temple leadership,
and judges. Joseph of Arimathea, who supplied Jesus' tomb, was
from this stratum. Caiaphas and Annas fit here as well.

(3) There was a far larger group who were peasants, land-owning farmers, and artisans. For them, life always was threatened by taxation and the fear of drought. They managed the sources of production for the economy and generated wealth that could be tapped by those in control. Many of them were desperately poor.

(4) Finally, there were the landless, the slaves, and the brigands (or criminals) who used violence, whether for gain or ideological reasons.

A quick look at Mark 6:21 (Herod's birthday party) or Matthew 20:25 demonstrates that characters from the top two strata are quite visible in the Gospels. And of course, we have to ask ourselves where Jesus fits in. He belonged to the third group, and because he was landless, unmarried, without an active trade, and without a permanent home, he would have been at its lower levels.

Now here is the striking thing. Jesus is utterly comfortable encountering those who live in the second stratum. He only has contact with the first stratum during his trial, when he meets the high priest Caiaphas, Pilate, and Herod Anti-

Christ in the House of Simon the Pharisee, Champaigne, Philippe de/Musee des Beaux-Arts, Nantes, France/Giraudon/The Bridgeman Art Library

A PAINTING BY PHILIPPE DE CHAMPAIGNE (1602–1674) DEPICTING THE STORY OF JESUS HAVING HIS FEET WASHED BY A "SINNER" WHILE IN THE HOME OF SIMON THE PHARISEE SHOWS THAT JESUS OFTEN INTERACTED WITH PEOPLE FROM ALL CLASS LEVELS.

pas. But we find numerous stories where Jesus—a man from the peasantry—is approached by someone with higher status. Jesus does not judge them nor does he refuse them. He listens to them and in some cases shows marked empathy. If we read the Gospels with some sensitivity to social status, surprising ideas emerge. An encounter with a "tax collector" takes on new importance. The presence of a Roman centurion is at once more complicated than we assumed.

JESUS AND THE POWERLESS

The cities of Galilee were not organized like our modern cities. Major Western cities (at least in the last fifty years) will often find the poor and powerless located near the urban center while more prosperous neighborhoods will be located either in the suburbs or in select renovated urban areas. Therefore, when we hear about a political candidate speaking in a tony neighborhood of Philadelphia, Detroit, or New York, we understand what is meant. *This is an upscale audience.*

But we also send codes of another sort. Everyone in Chicago knows what it means to be from the "west side." And when leaders such as Barack and Michelle Obama refer to their "southside roots," these are codes as well, sent to knowing ears. These are areas where significant numbers of the poor are found.

Ancient Galilee had its own codes. This region had its share of significant modern cities. And today archaeology has helped us understand Galilee's landscape with considerable clarity. Places like Sepphoris, Tiberius, and especially Greek Scythopolis would have been well-known to any distinguished Galilean visitor. But for the Jew, Sepphoris and Tiberius were most important. Sepphoris had always been the Jewish capital of Galilee, but it was destroyed and its population deported following an uprising in 4 BC. Herod Antipas rebuilt it to be a "jewel" in Galilee and also built nearby Tiberius on the lake as his second administrative center. These rebuilding efforts were well underway during Jesus' lifetime.

These two major cities of West Galilee known to Jesus, Sepphoris and Tiberius, likely had peak populations of around eight thousand. Sepphoris (north of Nazareth) has revealed villas comparable to those in Pompeii with vaulted rooms and

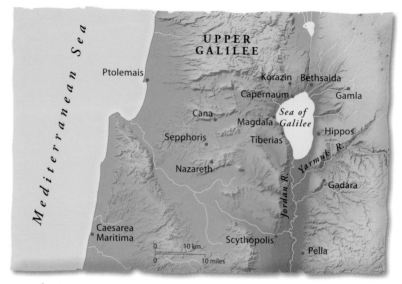

UPPER GALILEE

Mediterranean Sea

Ptolemais

Korazin   Bethsaida
Capernaum
Cana   Sea of
Magdala   *Galilee*   Gamla
Sepphoris   Tiberias   Hippos

Nazareth   Yarmuk R.

Jordan R.

Gadara

Caesarea
Maritima   Scythopolis
                                              Pella

0   10 km.
0   10 miles

| GALILEE AND SURROUNDING AREAS.

foundation stones that supported two and possibly three stories. Its street layout was organized around north/south, east/west intersecting boulevards (called, respectively, the *cardo* and the *decumanus*). The cardo was 43 feet wide (13 meters), with herringbone-patterned pavers and raised covered sidewalks, and it was lined with columns. Stores lined up between the columns on each side.

Todd Bolen/www.BiblePlaces.com

AERIAL VIEW OF BETH SHEAN (SCYTHOPOLIS) SHOWING THE OLD TESTAMENT TELL AND THE ROMAN CITY BELOW.

THE EXCAVATIONS OF THE GALILEE VILLAGE OF
TIBERIUS ON THE WEST SHORE OF THE SEA OF GALILEE.

Tiberius was built of black basalt stone. Less has been excavated here, but we can see the large southern gate to the walled city. It was guarded by two massive towers (23 feet [7 meters] in diameter) and opened on a cardo that was 40 feet wide (12 meters) and laid out also in a herringbone style. It too was lined with massive columns. In both cities mosaic floors decorated both public and private buildings.

COLUMNS REMAIN WHERE THEY HAVE
FALLEN IN ANCIENT SCYTHOPOLIS.

ANCIENT GERASA'S CENTRAL PUBLIC
BUILDINGS IN MODERN JERASH, JORDAN.

But the region had other spectacular cities as well—Greek cities that must have astounded the local peasant populations. The Greco-Roman designs found in Sepphoris and Tiberius showed up here on an even more massive scale. Here was public architecture with its columns, cardos (main streets), shops, theaters, and sports arenas. Scythopolis (Old Testament Beit

THE ROMAN TEMPLE AT PELLA, A MAJOR
DECAPOLIS CITY EAST OF THE JORDAN RIVER.

Shean) was a huge trading city, whose full extent (developed beyond the first century) is only now being excavated. Just to the east of Galilee (southeast of the lake), cities such as Gerasa and especially Pella and Gadara were standouts. These were urban centers that celebrated Greek culture, enjoyed the latest in architectural achievements, and had cosmopolitan populations. Their wealth was based on trade and the benefits of being economic centers for taxation in the area.

But where were the poor and the powerless? These cities were not for them. The poor were in the countryside. And this is where Jesus met the people he encountered.

Another generation of scholars once stereotyped rural Galilee as filled with the beleaguered poor—a population restless and angry with the urban elites in a place like Sepphoris. But this has now been clarified. Rural Galilee (and Judea) had numerous villages that hosted thriving economies. When pottery from the central Mediterranean appears in a village in central Galilee, you know someone there has money. When stoneware or olive oil is being shipped from rural areas to urban centers, there is active trade going on.

Therefore *outside* the cities there was a wide array of rural villages whose economies were dependent on Galilee's major

Todd Bolen/www.BiblePlaces.com

AGRICULTURE IN THE HILLS OF UPPER GALILEE
SURROUNDING HULEH LAKE.

THE FIRST-CENTURY SYNAGOGUE AT GAMLA.

cities. We have evidence of major Herodian farming estates in the region, but they existed on the periphery of Galilee, especially in the south (Jezreel Valley). The first-century historian Josephus talks about the hundreds of villages here. In his history of the Jewish war he writes that Galilee is "thick" with them (*Jewish War* 3.3.2; in his autobiography he refers to 204 villages, *Life* 235). Josephus also explains how the soil is so fertile that even lazy farmers could be successful! Today a short visit to Galilee bears this out. From Nazareth to the hills of Upper Galilee near Caesarea Philippi, the land is fertile and good for agriculture.

Some towns were fortified, such as the Jewish village of Gamla or Yodefat, which Josephus describes with

VERY LITTLE REMAINS OF THE WELL-KNOWN FIRST-CENTURY GALILEE VILLAGE OF YODEFAT.

some care (*Jewish War* 3.7.7). But most were unwalled and considerably more vulnerable. Towns like Capernaum, Chorazim, and Nazareth lacked walls and had populations of 1,000 to 1,500. Among the villages of Galilee, these were

ARTIST'S DEPICTION OF
THE CAPERNAUM HARBOR.

the least prestigious.

When Herod Antipas rebuilt Sepphoris (after its destruction) and began the construction of Tiberius, village life changed drastically. Suddenly, *within a generation*, a peasantry that once could sustain itself easily became a farming people paying hefty taxes and rents. Rapid population growth in these two cities required food and money, and the villages were made to supply them. Agriculture intensified (forests were removed and as much as 97 percent was farmed with fields and terraces), and some estimate that as much as one-third or one-half of all income went to taxes.

But why is this detour useful? If we scan through the Gospels, we gain a glimpse of where Jesus went, where he worked,

AN AERIAL VIEW OF SEPPHORIS, ONE OF THE CAPITAL
CITIES OF GALILEE DURING THE NEW TESTAMENT ERA.

and what he seems to avoid. *We possess no record of Jesus coming to the large urban centers of Galilee.* This explains why these major cities are unknown to the average reader; they are not mentioned in the New Testament. Of course, this may be an argument from silence: Jesus may have gone to these places, and we have no record of it. But their absence in the New Testament Gospels is striking to say the least. Villages are mentioned all around Tiberius, but Tiberius itself is not visited.

We have no record of Jesus in Sepphoris, although Jesus grew up about an hour's walk from the city. Tiberius is only mentioned once secondarily (John 6:23). What does this mean? This at least tells us that Jesus' ministry was focused on the village life of Galilee, where under Herod Antipas (the ruler during Jesus' adult life) tax burdens were severe, agricultural production stressed, and people held a keen sense of their powerlessness. This explains Jesus' remarks about paying taxes (Matt. 17:24; 22:17) and the forgiveness of debts (Matt. 6:12). It also raises the drama whenever Jesus has positive encounters with tax collectors themselves.

Jesus is moving among the powerless of his country. He is not in the ancient political or economic power centers. He is among those who are invisible to the leaders who control armies and palaces and the influential social structures of the day.

FAITH AND ENCOUNTER

Together these profiles of life in Galilee indicate to us that Jesus encountered a wide range of people. Some of these meetings were unexpected entirely. In the following pages I will survey a number of these encounters and take note of peculiar features of each encounter and explain cultural features that we might miss.

One initial note is necessary. Within Jesus' own world, complete with its ancient social organization, virtually every social strata and situation are represented. We find people with debilitating diseases, social isolation, and dubious careers. Some are wealthy. Some are poor. Some represent the mainstream of Jewish life. Others represent the margins—such as Samaritans or citizens of Tyre—whom the average rabbi would not generally meet.

One important idea resides here. *No situation or condition will impede Jesus' approach.* All are welcome, Jews and Gentiles alike. No poor decisions, no unethical behavior, no immoral history, and no irreligious attitudes make a difference. Jesus encounters people such as these from a wide spectrum of life, and he meets them where they live. He meets them at parties, on the streets, or in the synagogues. And as we will see, he is often criticized for his willingness to talk with them, encourage them, even to touch them (when society said not to touch).

This is a relief to those of us who are imperfect. Those of us who think about ourselves and the possibility of encountering Jesus should take strong comfort in it. Nothing in our lives or situations will be an impediment to him.

Chapter 2

THE WOMAN WITH THE HEMORRHAGE

Matthew 9:18–26; Mark 5:21–43

ON OCCASION, we can read a story in the Bible whose cultural values are completely foreign to us. They are difficult to understand because we share such little common ground.

In our modern society, we are sometimes shockingly casual about sexual intimacy. Blasé even. Visual media from magazines to film show explicit sexuality that we have become accustomed to. (I wonder how many times I've recommended a movie to college students and didn't remember whether there is a sex scene in it.) And yet, as a culture we are very private about something like female menstruation. I can mention sex in a class more easily than I can mention a woman's monthly period. Few teenage boys know what a tampon looks like.

Recently I was walking with my twenty-seven-year-old daughter through the old Arab markets of Hebron (in the West Bank). The place was crowded with people shopping and selling. Suddenly a young boy about twelve years old approached her and stuck in her hand a box of sanitary pads and asked my daughter for a price. We were surprised (to say the least) and had to laugh. Rarely in Chicago will young women get approached on the street by a vendor selling feminine hygiene supplies.

A BOAT MOSAIC THAT WAS FOUND AT MAGDALA.
www.HolyLandPhotos.org

What was going on here? In the ancient world of Judea (and much of the Middle East today) things were exactly the opposite from our world in these matters. Sex was intensely private, but female menstruation was quite public. And rules guiding the behavior of a woman who was "in her period" (or menses) would be well-known.

This is the sort of information we need in order to understand what happens when Jesus is touched by a "hemorrhaging woman." Cultural values are at work that we barely understand.

PRELUDE: PURE AND IMPURE

In one of the more ironic episodes in the Gospels, Jesus has just finished working on the east side of the Sea of Galilee. This region was called the Decapolis (Mark 9:20), which was a Greek

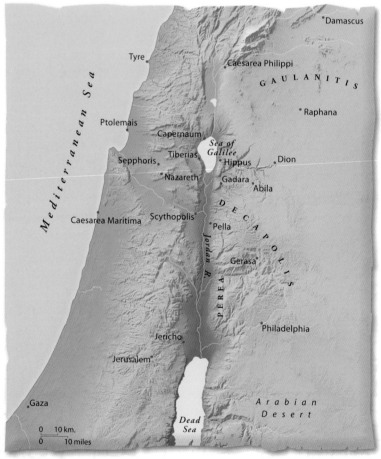

THE DECAPOLIS WAS A REGION OF HELLENISTIC
CITIES EAST OF GALILEE.

GADARA LIES ON THE CLIFFS ABOVE THE YARMUK RIVER
GORGE. THE SEA OF GALILEE CAN BE SEEN IN THE DISTANCE.

term for a confederation of ten cities (Gk. *deka*, ten; *polis*, city)
begun in the previous century. Roman armies in about 63 BC
had liberated these cities and promised them freedom from
Jewish rule. In Jesus' day they were centers of Hellenistic culture. The ruins of three of the most impressive cities—Gerasa,
Gadara, and Pella—are today standing in modern Jordan. To
get a sense of these cities, a visit to ancient Gadara on the cliffs
above the Yarmuk River gorge in Jordan sets the stage perfectly.

Here Jesus had freed a demon-possessed man and sent
the demons into a herd of swine. A Jewish reader of this story
would immediately be alarmed. Questions of impropriety
and impurity would quickly come to mind: this was Gentile
territory, here was a man living in a cemetery, he was demon-
possessed, and pigs were present. Each element introduces the
same problem. Jesus has been where Jews should not go: these
things were *unclean*.

When Jesus leaves the east side of the Sea of Galilee, he
returns to the "Jewish" regions in the west ("crossing to the
other side by boat"). This may have been a village like Magdala or Capernaum. But it was a fishing port, and when the
crowd gathers, Jesus is met by the ruler of the local synagogue.
His daughter is fatally ill—and she eventually dies. But as
Jesus heads to the man's home, he is met by a woman with a

A CEMETERY IN NEW TESTAMENT JERICHO. SUCH AREAS COULD BE VISITED BY FIRST-CENTURY JEWS BUT THEY WOULD MAKE A PERSON "UNCLEAN" AND REQUIRE SUBSEQUENT RITRUAL WASHING.

hemorrhage of blood who seeks healing. Again an ironic scene presents itself: a dead body and a flow of blood could likewise make Jesus *unclean*.

On both sides of the lake Jesus' approach is the same: his concern to provide mercy exceeds his concerns about ritual purity. That same day Jesus had said, "Go and learn what this means: 'I desire mercy, not sacrifice'" (Matt. 9:13). His compassion will override any rules for religious righteousness. He will always weigh need above ritual.

JESUS ENTERS THE VILLAGE

The scene in Mark 5:21 must have been typical. Jesus' reputation as a healer was spreading in Galilee, and his arrival in the village had caused a stir. He was a celebrity visitor. As an honored guest, the elders of the village would naturally come to greet him on behalf of everyone. These villages were small and often had far less than a thousand people. Surely the offer of a meal followed immediately and Jesus would accept, rendering honor to the village as he complimented its hospitality. A complete description of elder honoring takes place in Luke 19, when Jesus enters Jericho and surprises everyone by asking if he can join a tax collector for dinner.

However, in the present case, something irregular transpires. Jairus, the leader of the synagogue, is desperate. His daughter is critically ill (Gk. "at the point of death"),[1] and since Jesus is a known healer, Jairus asks for him to enter his home and treat her. This is a world where medicine was primitive and divine healing was expected. From antiquity we have numerous stories—both Jewish and Roman—describing the healing skills of many. And among these Jesus stood out. No magic formulae or incantations were used; his presence and word alone effected the change needed. Jesus agrees to follow Jairus and lay hands on the girl to heal her.

Mark likes stories that are (as scholars say) "sandwiched." That is, one story is interrupted by another so that the first story "frames" the second (see 3:20–35; 4:1–20; 5:21–43; 6:7–30; 11:12–21; 14:1–11; 14:17–31; 14:53–72; 15:40–16:8). Take Mark 11 as an example. Here Jesus (1) curses a fruitless fig tree; (2) cleanses the temple; and (3) returns to see the fig tree withered. The temple cleansing is "sandwiched" by two parts of the fig tree story. This sort of storytelling is common to Mark and adds to the drama and intrigue of what transpires. And I would suggest that the central story about the cleansing of the temple is the key story that Mark wants us to understand.

Here in Mark 5 we find the same literary form: (1) Jairus makes his request; (2) a woman is healed; and (3) Jairus's daughter is raised. And once again the story at the center is the key.

THE ENCOUNTER

Mark tells us that at once a crowd of people closes around Jesus as he begins walking with Jairus to his home. These are villages where little new happens, where most events are public, and where the arrival of an outsider—particularly one with a reputation—is noticed. But the parade is about to be interrupted.

A woman who has been ill for twelve years sees Jesus in the crowd, knows his reputation as a healer, and works her way forward. At once this poses a problem. First, early Judaism maintained strict boundaries between men and women. And in the present instance we can expect that the majority of people in the street are men. But for a woman to *touch* another man to whom she is not married—this is highly irregular. Such a woman would barely look at another man and rarely talk to a man not related to her family group.

The second problem is her illness. This problem, while not entirely debilitating, has continued for twelve years. And the language here no doubt points to uterine (or menstrual) bleeding and may possibly be cervical cancer. The Old Testament law placed strict boundaries around women who were in their monthly menstrual period or menses (Heb. *niddah*). In a word, they were unclean (or impure). This does not refer to personal hygiene. It refers to religious status because in this culture blood is sacred since it bears life, belongs to the domain of God, and so shifts the status of those who contact it. Leviticus provides some guidelines:

> *Anything she lies on during her period will be unclean, and anything she sits on will be unclean. Anyone who touches her bed will be unclean; they must wash their clothes and bathe with water, and they will be unclean till evening. Anyone who touches anything she sits on will be unclean; they must wash their clothes and bathe with water, and they will be unclean till evening. Whether it is the bed or anything she was sitting on, anyone who touches it will be unclean till evening.* (Lev. 15:20 – 23; see 15:19 – 31; 12:1 – 9)

A woman who had such an ongoing discharge was called *zabah* (or *zab*). The oral law (or Mishnah) took such situations so seriously it devoted one of its sixty-three tractates to "discharges" (Heb. *zabim*), regulating the rules that might apply in all cases where bodily discharges were present. A woman in this condition for twelve years would have found it socially crippling. Not only has this woman lost her money on physicians, but her life has amazing restrictions.[2] She should not touch others nor should she touch furniture others might use. Just touching her clothing would transfer her condition (Lev. 15:27; Mishnah, *Haggigah* 2.7). Since impurity could be passed from one person to another, food could not be shared; and in one tradition, water in the same room with her had to be covered. She was excluded from the temple and synagogue gatherings. If this started when she was young, she likely did not marry. And if she was married, it is likely she was divorced. This woman lived in a perpetual state of impurity, which resulted in her poverty, isolation, and suffering. The echo of "twelve" (she was ill for twelve years) reminds us of Jairus's daughter, who is twelve years old. She too is almost dead.

In the Roman world tremendous superstition surrounded menstruation. We do not know how widespread these views were, but they may give us a glimpse into popular thinking in the era. Pliny the Elder (or Gaius Plinius Secundus) lived in the mid-first century and wrote one of the most famous books of antiquity called

THE ENTRANCE TO THE FOURTH-CENTURY SYNAGOGUE AT CHORIZIM, A VILLAGE NEAR CAPERNAUM.

Natural History, which he dedicated to Emperor Titus in AD 77. In it he tried to catalogue all knowledge in a thirty-seven-book encyclopedia (geography in Books 1–6, human physiology in Book 7, insects in Book 11, medicine in Books 20–29); for our purposes he discusses menstruation in Book 28.

Pliny's remarks are astonishing. According to him, contact with the monthly "flow" of women turns new wine sour, makes crops wither, kills skin grafts, dries seeds in gardens, causes the fruit of trees to fall off, dims the bright surface of mirrors, dulls the edge of steel and the gleam of ivory, kills bees, and rusts iron and bronze. Dogs that come near become insane and their bite becomes poisonous. A thread from an infected dress is sufficient to do all of this. If linen that is being washed and boiled is touched by such a woman, it will turn black. A woman who is menstruating can drive away hailstorms and whirlwinds if she shows herself (unclothed) when lightening flashes. Pliny refers to Metrodorus of Scepsos in Cappadocia, who discovered that if a menstruating woman walks through a field while hold-ing the hem of her toga above her belt, "caterpillars, worms, beetles, and other vermin will fall from off the ears of corn." But, he warns, don't do this at sunrise or the crops themselves will die (*Natural History* 28.23).

I refer to Pliny only because he gives us a window into the magical, superstitious world of antiquity that had influenced Galilee for centuries. Romans who likely embraced these ideas lived in cities like Sepphoris, not far away. Simply put, this woman in Mark 5 has a condition that could fill any crowd with anxiety. And such anxieties only reinforced her isolation, her desperation, and her poverty.

The woman's strategy is also a crucial part of the story. She must take a risk to approach Jesus, and it is based on one vital idea: the status of "unclean" can be transmitted by touch. Since she is ritually unclean, as she moves through the crowd, she will make unclean every man she touches. But more, she has decided that if she touches Jesus, she can be healed—but at the same time, *she risks making him unclean!* Immediately a cry may go out. She will make impure the great honored guest of the village. It is like tossing ink on the garments of a dinner guest. She will shame herself—and more, she will shame the elders and the entire village. Jairus will be angry. This woman may be expelled from the town. This is her one toss of the dice.

THE "HEM" OF JESUS' GARMENT

In Jesus' day, men wore linen tunics that fell freely from the shoulder to the ankle. When at work, they would often belt the tunic around the waist and sometimes pull up the bottom hem and tuck it into the belt (John 21:7). Greek fashion had intro-duced the shorter knee-length toga (with high-laced sandals), but we suspect this appeared too immodest for Jews. At least we know that Jewish priests complained about such immodesty.

Religious Jewish men were distinguished by tassels or fringes (Heb. *tzitzit*) along the bottom hem of their tunic as required by the law (Num. 15:38–39; Deut. 22:12). These were strings that hung from each of four corners, which contained one blue thread reminding the wearer to obey the law. The practice of wearing a tasseled prayer shawl (Heb. *tallit*) only

A Byzantine mosaic showing Jesus with fringes on his tunic.

evolved in later Judaism after the second century, when the tunic was no longer in daily use.

We know that Jesus kept this practice and that people reached to touch his fringes in order to be healed (Matt. 14:36). As the tradition evolved, it became an ornament that quickly symbolized the wearer's authority or status. Jewish schools debated how long the tassels should be. Jesus complained about Pharisees who wore them to flaunt their status:

> Everything they do is done for people to see: They make their phylacteries wide and the tassels on their garments long; they love the place of honor at banquets and the most important seats in the synagogues; they love to be greeted with respect in the marketplaces and to have people call them "Rabbi." (Matt. 23:5–7)

The key here is that in this culture if the seat of authority is found in a rabbi's tunic fringes, to "grasp the fringe" is to reach for the power or authority resident in the wearer. In our story, the woman does not simply want to get Jesus' attention; she wants to benefit from any spiritual power that might be present with him. She reflects, "If I just touch his clothes, I will be healed" (Mark 5:28). Matthew, who is writing with keen Jewish sensitivities, tells the story more carefully: she touches the *edge* of his tunic (Matt. 9:20). When she does, at once she is healed.

The moment this happens Jesus stops, sensing that something significant has taken place. He looks around and asks, "Who touched my cloak?" Jesus has felt that power discharged from him. His question might be better translated, *Who has touched me and taken some of my power?* But in the midst of a crowd, everyone is touching; everyone is crushed together on the village street. Mark provides details that the other gospel writers abbreviate.

The drama of what happens next cannot be underestimated. Jesus and Jairus are surrounded by perhaps a hundred villagers, mostly men. The chatter and excitement build as the crowd of people makes their way to Jairus's home to watch a miraculous healing. And then—suddenly—everything stops. People stumble into each other trying to see what has happened. Jesus looks around. Something is wrong and the crowd is electrified by what it discovers.

This is when the woman steps forward. "Then the woman, knowing what had happened to her, came and fell at his feet and, trembling with fear, told him the whole truth" (Mark 5:33). I imagine the levels of fear in her are overwhelming. She is poor, sick, and "unclean," and now she has interrupted a dignified gathering hosted by the synagogue leader. And worse yet, she has touched the great visiting rabbi, who was their guest. The outrage of the crowd is likely tangible.

This encounter on a village road cries out for a resolution. Will Jesus judge her? Will he share in the crowd's anger? The woman has violated many social boundaries. Jesus was a famous teacher; she was poor and destitute. He was a righteous man; she was a woman plagued by impurity. Jesus breaks the silence and addresses her with the very title used by Jairus, "Daughter." Two daughters of Israel were ill that day. And Jesus was willing to heal both. "Daughter, your faith has healed you. Go in peace and be freed from your suffering" (Mark 5:34).

This restoration is not simply a medical healing for the woman. It is a complete restoration. It spells a reversal from a curse that brought with it tremendous social, religious, and, ultimately, personal implications. A woman who lived at the margin of village life is now—before the entire population—restored to a place she has not known for twelve years.

Jairus's Daughter

The healing of the hemorrhaging woman now permits the crowd to move on. But what has proved to be a miracle for the woman is a catastrophe for Jairus's daughter. The delay has cost her life. Immediately servants arrive from the ruler's home reporting that the girl has already died and that Jesus need not be bothered. The problem has now shifted. A healing miracle has now become more complex—will Jesus return life to a child who has died?

Surely the crowd is spellbound. There stands Jairus in the midst of his grief. There stands the woman who has delayed the crowd. And there stands Jesus, now seemingly incapacitated by this new report. As despair washes over Jairus, Jesus whispers, "Don't be afraid; just believe"(Mark 5:36). This is a word entirely unexpected. Fear always accompanies death; Jesus is about to shift that connection.

The same concerns that surrounded "impurity law" with the woman now return. A dead body was *unclean*, and to touch it by tending to its burial needs rendered a person ritually impure. The story has now fit a sequence of stories about Jesus and impurity: the cemetery-dwelling demoniac, the bleeding woman, and now the daughter each present Jesus with the same challenge: Will ritual impurity stop him?

A view of the village of Nain from the early twentieth century. In the distance, Mt. Tabor and nearby, Nazareth.

An ancient relief from the Old Testament era showing professional mourners. Such mourners attended the death of Jairus' daughter.

I imagine that by now, Jesus and the crowd have arrived near Jairus's home. Professional mourners are already at work. Cultural tradition required that families hire at least two flute players and at least one mourner.[3] But since Jairus was a man of some importance, numerous villagers have gathered to wail, cry, and dance grim sequences around the girl (much as it is done in nonwesternized Middle Eastern villages today).

But Jesus is not deterred. He tells the crowd to remain in the street, he dismisses the mourners, and he takes with him three of his followers (James, Peter, and John) with whom he had a more significant relationship. They would later accompany him also at the transfiguration (Mark 9:2), and eventually become vital leaders in the church. But here they will be witnesses, seeing and testifying to a resurrection that will presage the resurrection of Jesus himself.

"Why all this commotion and wailing? The child is not dead but asleep" (Mark 5:39). This remark inspires generous laughter. In Jesus' world, death could be referred to figuratively as sleep (see 1 Thess. 5:6, 10), and here Jesus employs it ironically (cf. John 11:13). Certainly all those present understand that the girl is truly dead. Six people remain around the girl's bed: her father, her mother, three disciples, and Jesus. Then Jesus *privately* speaks to the girl after he has taken her hand. His words are so significant that they were memorized in Aramaic when Mark wrote his Greek gospel: "*Talitha* [little girl] *koum* [arise]." And at once, the girl arises from her bed, walks, and eats, and everyone is filled with amazement.

The sheer length of this story, its many details, and its placement in Mark's gospel suggest that it became one of the premier miracles of Jesus. On another occasion near the Galilee village of Nain, Jesus had raised up a young man who had similarly died (Luke 7:11 – 17). And there the word about Jesus' powers spread like wildfire. In his final week, Jesus raised Lazarus from death (John 11), and news of this led to a plot on the lives of both Lazarus and Jesus (John 12:10). Therefore here Jesus tells the small circle to remain silent about what has transpired and to leave its elements ambiguous (Was the girl asleep after all? Was she merely unconscious?). But the parents knew and remembered — as did James, Peter, and John — and this story remained within the archived memory of Jesus' followers long after his own resurrection.

FAITH AND THE WOMAN

I have always been drawn to the character of the woman with the hemorrhage. The early church was as well. The Greek tradition named her Bernice. The Egyptian and Latin traditions named her Veronica.[4] But these are later attributions, and we cannot be sure of either of them. The earliest church historian, Eusebius (early fourth century), passed on a legend that she was from Caesarea Philippi and that by his day, a healing statue of her existed for the people in that city. Eusebius lived in the coastal city of Caesarea

Vanni/Art Resource, NY

A THIRD-CENTURY CARVING OF THIS STORY SHOWS THAT EVEN THE EARLY CHURCH WAS DRAWN TO THE CHARACTER OF THE WOMAN WITH THE HEMMORAGE.

Maritima and on a visit to northern Galilee he visited Caesarea Philippi and wrote the following:

> For they say that the woman with an issue of blood, who, as we learn from the sacred Gospel, received from our Savior deliverance from her affliction, came from this place [Caesarea Philippi], and that her house is shown in the city, and that remarkable memorials of the kindness of the Savior to her remain there.
>
> For there stands upon an elevated stone, by the gates of her house, a bold image of a woman kneeling, with her hands stretched out, as if she were praying. Opposite this is another upright image of a man, made of the same material, clothed decently in a double cloak, and extending his hand toward the woman. At his feet, beside the statue itself, is a certain strange plant, which climbs up to the hem of the brazen cloak, and is a remedy for all kinds of diseases.
>
> They say that this statue is an image of Jesus. It has remained to our day, so that we ourselves also saw it when we were staying in the city. (Church History 7.18.1–3)

I am not surprised that Christian imagination took hold of this woman's story. Seventeen hundred years ago people were venerating her memory and claiming healing at her home in Galilee. Her encounter with Jesus became a model for what it would mean for subsequent believers to meet Christ. Above all, she was bold, confident, living with abandon, and willing to take a risk—a social risk—in order to encounter the Lord. With the social pressure on her to remain invisible and on the margin, to disappear particularly when honorable society gathered, this pressure must have been enormous. Recall that she was *ritually unclean* and was prohibited public contact. Her movement through a crowd (chiefly made up of men) was risky in the extreme. And for her to touch Jesus exhibited an abandon and faith that are incomprehensible. She refused to see her condition as a

A RITUAL BATH (OR MIKVEH) FROM JERICHO.

ENCOUNTERS WITH JESUS

handicap. She refused to use her status as an excuse. She reached for Jesus' hem and threw caution to the wind.

But the story tells us also something about Jesus. *Ritual uncleanness did not affect him.* And this too is remarkable. In the first century, a righteous Jewish man would above all be alert to his religious status and would immediately take action if it were altered. Ritual baths (called a *mikveh*; plural *mikva'ot*) existed in every Jewish town to restore purity. The key here is that impurity only passed in one direction. An unclean person only passed his or her status to the clean—never the reverse. However, in Jesus' case the Jewish rule had no applicability. When Jesus had encounters with such people, *he passed clean to the unclean and not the other way around.* The woman's ritual status did not change him: his status changed her.

AIDS VICTIMS IN ZAMBIA ARE OFTEN SEEN AS "SOCIALLY UNACCEPTABLE" TODAY.

This alone is remarkable. Jesus is impervious and unaffected by any condition brought to him. Those in his society who might back away from the woman's condition would have difficulty comprehending Jesus and his willingness to touch and heal.

Which makes me think about my own society and the "unclean" boundaries we possess in a completely different sphere. I think of those who may be homeless or those who have AIDS or mental illness or any other socially judged disease, and I see the same reflexes in our world that existed toward this woman in her world. Jesus moved comfortably among those who were unclean. And today I am confident that he would do likewise.

Chapter 3

ZACCHAEUS OF JERICHO

Luke 19:1–10

DID JESUS really take an interest in those who were wealthy? Who knew how to invest shrewdly and prosper? We often reach for the one specific encounter he has with the rich "ruler" (Luke 18:18–23) and there note its tragic ending. Jesus challenges this man to divest himself of his wealth with the following result: "When he heard this, he became very sad, because he was very wealthy" (v. 23). But there are other hints that Jesus had a variety of contacts with the successful of Galilee. Among his supporters—his financial supporters—were women who came from Sepphoris or Tiberias and gave money to him (Luke 8:1–3).

Another hint is found in an overlooked story that is anchored in the ancient city of Jericho. Here lived a tax collector—no doubt a successful tax collector. And Jesus liked what he discovered in him.

TRAVELING TO JUDEA

Jesus traveled regularly between Galilee and Jerusalem during his lifetime. Every faithful Jew would do his or her best to make an annual pilgrimage to the temple, sometimes three

NEW TESTAMENT JERICHO DEVELOPED BY HEROD THE GREAT.
akg-images/Israelimages

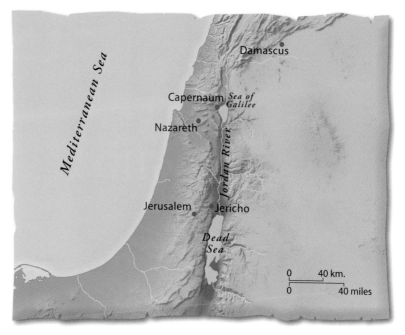

| TRAVEL ROUTE FROM THE SEA OF GALILEE TO JERUSALEM.

times each year for the major festivals. The route—just over a hundred miles—was well-known, and for safety people often traveled in groups. From the Sea of Galilee region, travelers generally moved south along the west side of the Jordan River just hugging the hills. Then after about eighty miles they would arrive at the splendid oasis of Jericho for rest and refreshment. From here the road climbed due west uphill into the mountains for another seventeen miles (and 3,600 feet of elevation), delivering them to Jerusalem. The poor walked. The wealthy might ride donkeys. The trip could take three or more days from Galilee on foot. The steep walk from Jericho to Jerusalem along the Roman road required about seven hours.

This route explains why Jesus returned to Jericho so many times. It was a waypoint for pilgrims moving north and south. And the trip from there up to the temple could be dangerous. This was the setting of Jesus' parable of the good Samaritan (Luke 10:30), whose victim was walking on this same road (see chapter 4). The Samaritan rescued the man by placing him on his own donkey (10:34) and taking him to a Jericho inn for assistance.

THE STEEP ROMAN ROAD FROM JERICHO TO JERUSALEM.

Because of Jericho's commercial agricultural value, in antiquity the city was a royal estate for two hundred years. Its spring (Arabic: the *Ein es-Sultan*) was strong and today it irrigates over 2,500 acres. Together Jericho's abundant water, rich alluvial soil, and twelve months of sunshine produced rich harvests of balsam and palm and won it the name "City of Palms."

Jericho was also valuable strategically. Fortresses could close this vital eastern corridor to Jerusalem. When Rome conquered the area in 63 BC, Pompey destroyed three Jewish forts here. But soon the region was rebuilt. Mark Antony (the close ally of Julius Caesar) admired Jericho and gave it

JERICHO'S PALM TREES WERE FAMOUS THROUGHOUT THE EASTERN MEDITERRANEAN.

SWIMMING COMPLEX IN HEROD'S
NORTHERN PALACE AT JERICHO.

HEROD'S FORTRESS OF
CYPRUS ABOVE JERICHO, NAMED
AFTER HEROD'S MOTHER.

as a gift to his lover, the Egyptian Cleopatra. In Jesus' day the oasis was rented to the Herodian families.

In the New Testament era, Herod the Great built for himself a winter palace in Jericho where he could retire from the cold, wet winters in Jerusalem. Here in the desert a thousand feet below sea level, winter heat was abundant. The palace had beautiful baths and a swimming complex that made guests compare it with Pompeii. Above it he built a walled fortress for protection and named it after his mother, Cyprus.[5] Today both the fortress and Herod's winter villa are open but rarely visited (see the aerial view of Jericho, p.54).

This is a useful profile when we reconstruct ancient New Testament Jericho. This was not a sleepy rural village. Despite its remote location in the eastern desert, it thrived thanks to its oasis and its placement. Money moved through the city regularly. Trade from the east that moved west into the Judea highlands passed through Jericho; as a result, the town became a tax station. It would not have been uncommon to find expansive villas built here much like the palace of Herod. They had pools, baths, tiled courtyards lined with columns, plastered

The fortress of Cyprus, viewed from Jericho.

frescoes, and countless palm trees. Two thousand feet south of the city archaeologists have discovered an elongated oval race track (a hippodrome) used for horses and chariots; attached to it at the north was a theater. For Jews coming here for the winter months, Jericho may have been an entertainment center as well. But religion was not neglected. Jewish ritual baths and—most important—the remains of a first-century synagogue have all been found.

This is the world of Zacchaeus, Jericho's tax collector.

A typical Roman villa in Italy.

Fresco of a dove from Pompeii

MOSAIC LOCATED IN THE FIRST-
CENTURY SYNAGOGUE AT JERICHO.

THE ENCOUNTER

The story of Jesus' final departure from Galilee is a sober
account. It is punctuated with Jesus' predicting his arrest
in Jerusalem and the disciples' frightened response (Luke
18:31–34). As he walks from southern Galilee (17:11) toward
Jericho, he encounters numerous people who know his reputation and wish to make contact. Lepers meet him in search of
healing (17:12). Parents bring their children to him so he might
touch them (18:15). A wealthy man—a Jewish ruler—stops him
and asks about eternal life (18:18). As he enters Jericho, a blind
man sitting on the road calls out to him and asks for restored
sight (18:35). There is a sense of urgency in the story. This will
be Jesus' last trip this way. He is a man on a quest. And Jerusalem is his final destination.

Jesus' arrival in the village of Jericho must have come with
considerable fanfare. By then his public ministry is almost
complete. He has visited countless villages throughout Galilee,
and no doubt those who heard him carried stories of healing
and exorcism south to places like Jericho and the villages near
Jerusalem. His pronouncements about the kingdom of God
were carefully noted by the ruling authorities, and those in
power were already watching him carefully.

We can imagine, then, that he does not slip into Jericho quietly. His reputation has preceded him. And when he heals the blind man at the city's outskirts and the crowd witnesses it, news of this spreads quickly. The blind man — known to most — follows Jesus into town praising God (Luke 18:43).

Z. Radovan/www.BibleLandPictures.com

HEROD'S WINTER VILLA IN JERICHO.

Todd Bolen/www.BiblePlaces.com

THE REMAINS OF THE FIRST-CENTURY SYNAGOGUE, JERICHO.

Todd Bolen/www.BiblePlaces.com

THE HERODIAN HIPPODROME (HORSE RACE TRACK) IN JERICHO.

But this is also a momentous occasion, filled with drama: Jesus of Nazareth is not simply a popular teacher. He is a man of considerable controversy. Herod in Galilee wants him killed (Luke 13:31), and recently Jesus told scandalous stories about the rich and the well-placed (Luke 15:25 – 32; 16:19 – 31). He has also been talking publicly about his own demise in Jerusalem (18:31 – 34). Clearly a crisis is brewing.

We have already explored the significance of public receptions and honoring in Jesus' culture (see chapter 2). As Jesus enters Jericho, a crowd has already formed (Luke 19:3), and we can assume that within it, the elders of the community have also gathered. Children running in the streets have passed the word; soiled tunics have been exchanged for fresh ones;

women have begun planning the day's menu and giving orders to servants.

The expectations and roles of everyone are clear: Jesus will be met by the elders, he will be escorted to a villa, and there he will be welcomed with foot washing, food, beverages, congenial conversation, and rest. These are *honoring gestures*, and they contribute to the honor not only of the elders but the entire community. The crowds of people lining Jericho's main road understand their place and the role of the elders to whom Jesus is walking.

One thing is certain. Zacchaeus is not among them.

ZACCHAEUS THE TAX FARMER

In the province of Judea, the Romans permitted the Jerusalem temple authorities to run much of the civil administration of the country. This meant a direct tax was levied on people by the Jewish leadership. A so-called annual "temple tax" required a half shekel to be paid to the temple treasury by every man (Matt. 17:24; cf. Ex. 30:11 – 16). This was generally collected at Passover. Yet many (such as the Sadducees) disputed this tax as a recent invention, and the Jews at the Qumran settlement paid it only once in their lifetime. Compliance may have been seen as a matter of patriotism or loyalty, not a legal obligation.[6]

In addition "land taxes" were collected in the form of tithes. Ten percent of a family's income was given to the temple (Lev. 27:30 – 33), much of which was used for the Levites who served it (Num. 18:21). There is evidence that the temple also expected a "second tithe" of what remained, though some scholars dispute this. The oral law devoted an entire tractate to it (Mishnah,

Photo: Clara Amit, courtesy Israel Antiquities Authority

A HALF-SHEKEL COIN, JUDEA.

Ma'aser Sheni), but its application in Jesus' day is uncertain. At best, it may have been a tithe used for personal festival celebration inside Jerusalem. Either way, these land taxes were not for Jewish ministry; they were national taxes to run the country and in particular, Jerusalem.

AN AERIAL VIEW OF THE FIRST-CENTURY SYNAGOGUE RECENTLY UNCOVERED AT MAGDALA IN GALILEE (A NORTHERN TAX CENTER).

Roman taxes were a separate matter. Rome valued conquered provinces as sources of revenue. The Jewish historian Josephus estimated that Herod Antipas's tax debt to Rome just for the region of Galilee was 1.2 billion denarii annually.[7] Here they targeted the production value of the region as well as individuals in it (Mark 12:13 – 17).[8] Caravans of Jewish olive oil (or products like salted fish, fruit, pottery, or salt) moving toward the Mediterranean for shipment had to pay. Therefore tolls and customs taxes on any merchandise transiting through the country were their interest. They created tax districts and within them designated collection points. Capernaum in Galilee was one of these (which is why Matthew the tax collector was there, Matt. 9:9). Other taxing centers (Gk. *toparchoi*) were Jerusalem, Gaza, Ashkelon, Joppa, Sepphoris, Gabara, Tarichaeae (called Magdala), and Caesarea. Jericho was also a tax center.[9]

At these locations Rome sold the right to collect these taxes to the highest bidder, sometimes called a "tax farmer." Rome

THE SITE OF MAGDALA ON THE SEA OF GALILEE WAS ALSO A
ROMAN TAXING CENTER FOR FISH PRODUCTS FROM THE SEA.

set a revenue target for the region; the investor guaranteed this
amount and was then permitted to charge any amount above
the tax as profit. The possibilities for fraud and abuse were
obvious, and the Roman Senate regularly raised concerns.
This exploitation accounts for the sheer public disdain for toll
collectors. The Jewish law called them "thieves," and the public
often compared them with sinners (Matt 11:19) and Gentiles
(Matt. 18:17). They were often unscrupulous, their efforts were
backed by the Roman army, and as a result they held extremely
low status. John the Baptist once warned them to take only what
was appropriate (Luke 3:12 – 13).

Zacchaeus lived in Jericho and was its "chief tax collector"
(Gk. *architelônçs*). He owned the tax district and had subordi-
nates who worked for him collecting money. We can assume
that Zacchaeus was wealthy, we know he was a Jew (Luke 19:9),
and we know that he did not enjoy the respect of the community (19:7). He worked closely with the army that occupied the
land, and because he had regular contact with Gentiles through
the Roman tax network, he was considered unclean. Tax collectors rarely went near the temple for worship. The rabbis taught
it was even acceptable to dislike their families.

When Jesus enters Jericho, he causes such a stir that even
Zacchaeus is aware of it. The crowd forms, the elders move

together with great dignity to greet Jesus, and Zacchaeus is not invited to join the hosting party. This is a mark of his status. Zacchaeus is despised and excluded. Many hate him.

Luke's story says that because Zacchaeus is short of "$h\varsigma likia$," he cannot see past the crowd (Luke 19:3). Many have concluded that this Greek term refers to his shortness of height and that the crowd is a visual obstacle (TNIV, "because he was short he could not see over the crowd"). However, $h\varsigma likia$ refers only to "stature" and so may refer to age (Zacchaeus is young), height, or social status. Many believe the latter is most likely. The crowd, in other words, doesn't become a visual obstacle (we should not imagine Zacchaeus jumping up and down behind taller onlookers) as much as it becomes a social obstacle. The sense is: Zacchaeus cannot see Jesus and his troupe because he is despised, and the crowds make no room for him.

But Zacchaeus is a resourceful man. Rather than push his way through, he climbs a nearby sycamore tree, stands in its branches, and watches. The irony of the scene must have been amazing. A man of short stature *climbs* to gain height, and a man who views himself as powerful takes huge risks to gain access to Jesus. Why? Men wearing tunics do not climb trees like children. The risk of ridicule is tremendous.

THE SYCAMORE TREE RECALLING ZACCHAEUS PLANTED IN JERICHO DURING THE BRITISH MANDATE ERA (1920–1948).

JESUS AND ZACCHAEUS

Jesus no doubt meets the elders, is greeted warmly, and continues to walk into Jericho. At this point the scene takes an unexpected turn. Before formal invitations from the elders can be uttered, Jesus stops, he looks up into the sycamore tree behind the crowd, and he calls Zacchaeus by name. "Zacchaeus, come down immediately. I must stay at your house today" (Luke 19:5). These are words no one expected to hear.

We should not underestimate the shock this has on the crowd. People of high stature have suddenly been bypassed. Elders whose homes are being burnished to perfection for the visitor now stand dumbfounded. Protocol has been wrecked. Hard questions are being asked at once; Jesus does not seem to understand appropriate conduct. He doesn't understand that righteous men should socialize only with others who are equally righteous. But he is going to linger in the home of an unrighteous man.

Immediately Zacchaeus climbs down, breaks through the stunned crowd, and approaches Jesus. "He ... welcomed him gladly" (19:6), which means they exchange kisses and honoring greetings and begin to walk together. It is remarkable that Jesus knows his name. Zacchaeus is not invisible, but known. He is not despised by this visitor, but publicly received. A man literally on the margin has now been brought inside. And those who enjoy public prestige daily are left standing alone and dishonored.

It only takes moments for the derision to begin. The crowd murmurs immediately and audibly: Jesus cannot apparently discern the difference between righteous and unrighteous—he prefers to be with sinners than with honorable leaders of Jericho. This reaction requires some explanation. Jesus' culture was deeply concerned with honor and shame. Life was orchestrated around preserving honor and avoiding shame at all costs. This was how social status was measured. In this case, the Jericho crowd believes that Jesus has shamed either the town or its elders. He has spurned established protocols for honoring. In order to regain honor, the crowd impulsively shames Jesus in return. Their disparaging remarks—loud enough for everyone to hear—are aimed to damage Jesus and

Zacchaeus while restoring the elders' stature. To dishonor Jesus is to remove the shame now encircling the elders in the street.

But both Jesus and Zacchaeus hear it and will not let it pass.

ZACCHAEUS THE RIGHTEOUS

If there ever was a moment of village drama, this moment qualifies richly. Jesus and Zacchaeus walk to the tax collector's richly appointed home—the elders left behind in a publicly shaming condition—while the crowd moves in more tightly, growing louder as they utter rude things to both of them. When Jesus stops and turns, everyone expects a small conflict. How will Jesus reverse the impact of these remarks? How can he restore his honor? How might he justify himself? Or is he something unimaginable: a man who disregards shame?

That Zacchaeus speaks first is a mark of his real stature. He does not wait for Jesus to mount a defense and rescue him. But sadly, in the history of interpretation his words have been often misconstrued. The TNIV translates, "Look, Lord! Here and now I give half of my possessions to the poor, and if I have cheated anybody out of anything, I will pay back four times the amount" (Luke 19:8). These words from this translation appear as a pledge, a promise to repent and reform. As such they compare with Jesus' word to the rich young ruler in the previous chapter (18:22): "You still lack one thing. Sell everything you have and give to the poor, and you will have treasure in heaven. Then come, follow me." Zacchaeus is now committed to the very thing the rich young ruler was not. Zacchaeus understands the values of justice and care of the poor. These words confirm the call of the crowd that Zacchaeus was and is "a sinner," but now thanks to Jesus things will be different.

But this is not what Zacchaeus says. His comment to Jesus is in the present tense. "Look! I give half of my possessions, Lord, to the poor. And if I have defrauded anyone, I repay them fourfold." Greek has what we call the "future use" of the present tense, and interpreters sometimes apply it here. But this is not demanded. Generally these uses imply some immediacy or certainty, such as Revelation 22:20, where the Lord says, "I am coming soon." This too is in the present tense but with a *future* meaning.[10]

But many scholars refuse to use it here in Luke 19. We have no suggestion that Zacchaeus needs to repent, nor does the story imply any conversion on his part. He even refers to Jesus as "Lord," a term of high honor and discipleship in Luke. As Joel Green remarks, "On this reading Zacchaeus does not resolve to undertake new practices but presents for Jesus' evaluation his current behaviors regarding money."[11]

This would be a great revelation to the electrified audience standing on the street in Jericho. *Zacchaeus is not what everyone has assumed.* He has been honest; he is collecting what is demanded without corruption and abuse, and he is generously giving away large portions of his wealth. The law required that if there was financial fraud, the original amount had to be returned plus 20 percent (Lev. 6:5). Here Zacchaeus practices fourfold reimbursement.

When word of this emerges outside, the crowd that thought it had seen one shocking scene for the day now witnesses another. Their notorious tax farmer, who has colluded with the Romans, is a man of principle. Rumors of his corruption are evaporating like a mist.

This is when Jesus speaks up. "Today salvation has come to this house, because this man, too, is a son of Abraham. For the Son of Man came to seek and to save what was lost" (Luke 19:9–10). Jesus has found a man whose heart is ready for his kingdom, who loves God and lives righteously, who distributes his wealth for the care of the poor. And he is deeply misunderstood, living on the social margin of this Jewish town. Jesus announces that just such a man belongs to his kingdom.

Jesus vindicates Zacchaeus with two statements for the crowd to digest. First, salvation has come to Zacchaeus's house. The word "salvation" does not refer to Zacchaeus's eternal destiny, as if it were an evangelistic idiom. This word refers to restoration and rescue. Zacchaeus is being restored to his honor within the community because Jesus is going to be in his home. Note the parallel language: "I must stay at your house *today*" (19:5), and "*today* salvation has come to this house" (19:9). Here is a Jew in whom the values of the kingdom are already at work.

This word is then followed quickly by another: Zacchaeus is a son of Abraham. Here Jesus gives a second affirmation. This word is not a revelation to Jericho that Zaccheus was Jewish. That was obvious to all. Here Jesus has done more. He has reminded them that Zaccheus has embodied a life characteristic of God's people. Jesus will not deny—and he challenges the crowd to do the same—that Zaccheus is one of them, a Jew, a community member, a righteous man.

Zaccheus's name is actually a Greek form of a famous Hebrew name: Zakkai. This well-known name appears frequently in Jewish texts from the period. Its root is found in the Hebrew word *tzâdaqa* [stem: *tzdq*], which occurs over five hundred times in the Old Testament. *Tzâdaqa* means righteousness. Therefore Zakkai means *righteous*. And this introduces the final irony to this story. Jericho's tax farmer has now been discovered to be the very thing his name implied. This, then, is the justification of Jesus' moving into the home of a tax collector—a sinner's occupation according to the crowd. Jesus is on a quest to locate those who have been lost, who need to be restored and drawn back into the community to which they belong.

This is where Zaccheus's story ends. We do not know what happens next. I imagine that Jesus and Zaccheus have a long afternoon talking about Jericho, and Rome, and careers. But the gospel is (perhaps) mercifully silent about what transpires. Nor do we know the reaction of the crowd and its elders. On that Passover are they among the thousands cheering Jesus on Palm Sunday? This occurs within days (Luke 19:28–40). Are Jericho's elders among those interrogating Jesus about Roman taxes in Jerusalem (Luke 20:19–26)? Or do they join the ranks of those calling for his crucifixion five days later (Luke 23:20)?

FAITH AND ZACCHAEUS

Zaccheus's encounter with Jesus in Jericho is striking on many levels. It tells us, for instance, about Jesus' willingness to find disciples in what appear to be unlikely places. Jesus moves to the social margin, *precisely* where people of unscrupulous character may live. And there he locates a man about whom both the public and the religious leadership have been wrong. In other words, Jesus bypasses those who think that they are the appropriate recipients of God's grace and reaches for those

AN ARAB BANQUET FROM THE
NINETEENTH CENTURY SHOWING THE
IMPORTANCE OF PUBLIC HOSPITALITY.

who often think of themselves as unreach-able. Jesus finds his disciples in trees, not in prestigious gatherings of the religiously content.

I am also intrigued with the risks Jesus has taken. To associate with a tax collec-tor and still maintain that you are a good and righteous man strains the reasoning of any audience.

Jesus' announcement ("I must stay at your house!") implies that he will share a meal there. And in Jesus' culture this is explicit code for social acceptance and hospitality.

Imagine any pastor being good friends with a socially despised person holding a disrespected vocation. Now imagine them playing golf every week and the picture becomes clear. Jesus' own reputation is at risk, and yet he values the discov-ery of Zacchaeus beyond the preservation of his own name. Conservative religious communities are rarely like that. They frequently preserve themselves by avoiding the public stain of inappropriate associations.

But it is the profile of Zacchaeus that stands out. Here is a man of quiet faith who himself is on a quest to encounter Jesus. He too takes risks. And he has been pressed to the margins of his world by the very people to whom he ought to belong. He is a businessman. He is pragmatic. Wealthy. Well connected among the powerful. And yet—which is where the surprises begin—Zacchaeus is honest instead of corrupt; he is generous rather than greedy; he understands distribution as well as accumulation, and he is interested in people (the poor), not simply prosperity.

It seems clear that as Jesus nears Jericho and continues to Jerusalem, questions of wealth and power become important. Jesus' conversation with the rich ruler and its aftermath (Luke 18:18–30) invite an immediate comparison with Zacchaeus later. Both men are "rulers" and are wealthy. The first says he keeps the commandments; Zacchaeus is called a sinner. The first falls away when Jesus tells him to rethink his relationship to wealth; Zacchaeus is already letting go of it.

This is why Jesus immediately recognizes here a true "son of Abraham" who needs to be brought back into the fold of the kingdom and rejoined to its purposes. Zacchaeus is not a bad man who is converted; he is a good man who is discovered, affirmed, and welcomed. And in that encounter with Jesus, certainly what he knows implicitly about his faith now will become explicit. Jesus has shared a meal with him a week before his death and surely Zacchaeus will never forget it.

Chapter 4

THE CENTURION OF CAPERNAUM

Luke 7:1–10

WE ARE ambivalent about Jesus' connection to people of power. For many interpreters, Jesus lived and worked among those who were powerless—in particular, the poor. And when we think about the "powerful" of Judea, we only recall his confrontations with Pilate, Caiaphas, and Herod Antipas, three men with overt antagonism toward him. These scenes occurred at the end of his life when tensions were acute and a conspiracy was well underway to arrest and kill him.

Certainly Jesus (like us) knew people for whom brokering power was central to their identity. They had gained the respect (or fear) of the population and were well positioned. This raises an interesting set of questions that has an immediate applicability. *Did Christ avoid the powerful? Did he engage them? Was he intimidated by them?* One unusual story from Capernaum—a story about a career military officer—may provide us with some clues.

ANCIENT CAPERNAUM

Capernaum was a small, unwalled fishing village on the north shore of the Sea of Galilee. This sea is a large freshwater lake

---

GOLD AUREUS OF OCTAVIAN, REFERRING TO CAESAR.

(about 7 miles wide, 12 miles long) fed by the Upper Jordan River in the north and having an outlet in the south (the Lower Jordan). The name *Capernaum* comes from Hebrew: "village (*kfar*) of Nahum." The village flourished in this region because freshwater springs abound at the bottom of the northwest area of the lake, and fish gather there in greater density. Many such villages have been located all around the lake; at present we have remains of these. Magdala was one — as were Sennabris, Hippos, Susita, Tabgha, Ein Gofra, and Aish, village ports not mentioned in the New Testament. Capernaum may have been settled in the second century BC since few archaeological remains have surfaced from earlier periods.[12]

Fishing villages like this were common in Galilee; in fact fish were a critical part of the country's economy. Jerusalem, for instance, had a "Fish Gate" (Neh. 3:3). *Bethsaida* means "house of fish." Magdala was also called *Tarichaeae*, which means "fish processing." A *migdal* (hence Magdala) was a tower where salted fish were stacked and prepared for shipment. Even many of Jesus' disciples fished for a living.

FISH FROM THE SEA OF GALILEE.

ENCOUNTERS WITH JESUS

www.HolyLandPhotos.org

FALLEN GRANITE COLUMNS TOPPLED DURING AN
EARTHQUAKE AT HIPPOS (SUSITA), A ROMAN CITY
ON THE EAST SIDE OF THE SEA OF GALILEE.

Today Capernaum is a ruin (and has been so for almost a
thousand years), but thanks to the quick work of the Catholic
Franciscans in the nineteenth century, the site was fenced and
preserved. Today visitors can see the remains of a Jewish synagogue that was built in the fourth century AD, many monumental remnants of that later village on display in the gardens,
and remarkable excavations of the village's first-century black
basalt residences. This basalt level was the community known
to Jesus. Part of
its residential
quarter and cem-
etery are there to
see. And beneath
the floor of the
white fourth-
century syna-
gogue we have the
foundations of
the earlier black
synagogue, well-
known to Jesus.

Z. Radovan/www.BibleLandPictures.com

CAPERNAUM SYNAGOGUE WITH THE
FIRST-CENTURY FOUNDATION OF
BLACK BASALT AND FOURTH-CENTURY
WHITE LIMESTONE WALLS.

A MODEL OF A FIRST-CENTURY BOAT AT EIN GEV
ON THE EAST SHORE OF THE SEA OF GALILEE.

JESUS IN CAPERNAUM

Jesus moved to Capernaum after his tragic rejection at Nazareth (Luke 4:16–30). When he was at this coastal village, people said he was at "home" (Mark 2:1). It was in Capernaum that Jesus met some of his most prominent disciples, such as

AERIAL VIEW OF CAPERNAUM ALONG THE SEA OF GALILEE'S
NORTHWEST SHORE. THE WELL-KNOWN EXCAVATION OF
CAPERNAUM IS TO THE LEFT (NOTE THE WHITE SYNAGOGUE).

James and John. Peter and Andrew lived there even though they had originally come from Bethsaida (John 4:44). We know that to increase profits, families formed "cooperatives" (or guilds, Greek *koinônoi*), and their partners (*metochoi*) shared nets and boats (see Luke 5:7–10, where guild language is used). The Zebedee family probably owned such a cooperative (or worked for one), and this was the circle that Jesus befriended.

FISH NET WEIGHTS FROM THE SEA OF GALILEE USED DURING ANTIQUITY.

Capernaum's synagogue witnessed Jesus' first exorcism (Mark 1:21–28). Many miracles were done here (1:29–33). In fact, as Jesus' "base" of ministry, many of his efforts were centered among three villages that formed a triangle on the sea's north shore: Capernaum, Chorazin, and Bethsaida. This was where Jesus gave the "Sermon on the Mount" and where he fed the five thousand. It is no wonder that Jesus had high expectations for the Jews living there and was publicly critical of their lack of faith (Matt. 11:21).

But coming to Capernaum was also a strategic decision. This village was

MANY OF JESUS' DISCIPLES MADE THEIR LIVING AS FISHERMEN.

THE HILLSIDE ABOVE CAPERNAUM WHERE JESUS MAY HAVE DELIVERED THE SERMON ON THE MOUNT.

ideal for reaching the many people who were moving through the region regularly. Capernaum lay on part of a vital highway (the famed *Via Maris* or "way of the sea") that connected central Galilee with the north. This was not a major international corridor, but a local route—which explains why Capernaum had no public buildings

A ROMAN MILE MARKER ALONG THE FAMOUS *VIA MARIS* (WAY OF THE SEA) IN JUDEA.

or monumental architecture.[13] Moreover, the village was poor. Homes there show none of the fine building detail we see at Sepphoris. The people likely had stone walls and suspended wood/thatch roofs.[14]

Trade moving from central Galilee and on north to Damascus had to navigate around the Sea of Galilee. Caravans traveled north to the top of the sea, turned east, and then went north again, following the hills until the road climbed to the Golan plateau. Therefore many people moved through Capernaum, and this gave it high value as a trade center.

Rome noted this. Thus for them, it became a tax center. Once a caravan crossed the northern Jordan River (where the river enters the sea), it crossed into another tax district run by Herod Philip. To capture revenue effectively, Herod Antipas (the ruler of Galilee) made Capernaum his net for pulling in tax monies moving either east or west across his frontier. Matthew (the tax

ONE OF THE NORTHERN TRADE ROUTES TRAVELED THROUGH CAPERNAUM.

| BLACK BASALT FIRST-CENTURY HOMES EXCAVATED IN ANCIENT
CAPERNAUM.

collector) lived there and later would become Jesus' disciple
(Matt. 9:9). When Jesus was in Capernaum, it is not surprising
that many tax collectors contacted him (9:10), and he social-
ized with them (11:19; Luke 15:1).

Such an economic choke point for the region also brought
the military, which enforced imperial taxation policies
and policed the population. This is undoubtedly why, in
one unlikely story, Jesus encounters a Roman centurion in
Capernaum.

A NINETEENTH-CENTURY CARAVAN RECALLS
THE COUNTLESS CARAVANS THAT MOVED THROUGH
THE MIDDLE EAST FOR CENTURIES. |

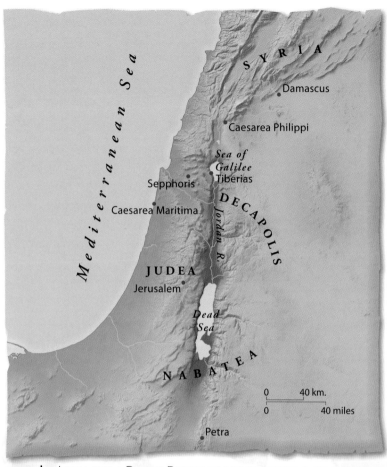

Sea of Galilee

DECAPOLIS

NABATEA

JUDEA WAS A ROMAN PROVINCE AND PROVIDED A STRATEGIC
CONNECTION BETWEEN EGYPT AND SYRIA.

ROMAN OCCUPATION

In a sweeping campaign that was as quick as it was successful,
Rome conquered Israel in 63 BC during a period of internal
turmoil in Jerusalem. No siege of Jerusalem was required. The
city simply surrendered. Under the leadership of a general
named Pompey, the territory was easily suppressed, reorgan-
ized into an imperial Roman province, and given the name
Judea (from the Greek word *Ioudaioi*, referring to the Jews who
lived there). Rome gave Judea a free hand in governing itself so
long as there were no uprisings and tax revenues were uninter-
rupted. Rulers from the Jewish Herodian dynasty (so named
after the family of Herod) controlled the country for many
years throughout the New Testament period, but from 4 BC for-

ward (the death of Herod the Great) Roman military presence throughout the country increased.

For Rome, Judea was not only a tax asset; it was a strategic asset. Judea controlled a vital corridor linking Egypt with Syria—two more critical provinces. And just to the east of Syria was Persia, Rome's continual nemesis. Therefore Rome strengthened the country, carefully building its own garrisons and making sure that a series of forts built by Herod would always be at its disposal. Since Rome gave the Jews relatively free reign, no major military units (called legions) were kept in Judea. The nearest garrisoned legions were in Syria and Egypt.

Rome's army was unmatched for its sophistication and organization. This was a highly disciplined, professional fighting force. It used modern tactics, cavalry support, engineering, and excellent supply trains, and it could build siege engines to assail any city. It was mobile and could move throughout the empire on ships or along an extensive network of expertly engineered roads. The army was built around a series of "legions." These were organizational units (like military brigades) that consisted of about 4,800 infantry (plus supply corps, engineers, and cavalry). Ideally the legion was subdivided into ten "cohorts" that each had 480 legionnaires. And these cohorts were again divided into "centuries" of eighty men each. Each century was led by an officer called a centurion. Centurions would organize their centuries into teams of eight, who would share a mule, a tent, and cooking.

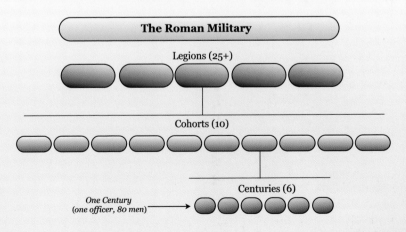

A REENACTOR SHOWS HIS DETAILED ROMAN CENTURION UNIFORM.

THE HELMET OF A LEGIONNAIRE SOLDIER.

THE HELMET OF A CENTURION.

The centurion was the backbone of the army. These were professional soldiers who served on average about twenty years and had their own internal rankings. Many came up through the ranks and took ten to fifteen years to become centurions. Some transferred from the emperor's personal guard (the Praetorian Guard). They could be recognized by their uniform. Ordinary infantry wore crested helmets with the crest running front to back. Centurions wore helmeted crests side to side and carried a traditional vine branch called a *vitis* (*bacillum viteum*) as a symbol of their authority. When the army shifted to solid armor, the centurions retained the old-fashioned chain mail to suggest their invincibility. They could also be accompanied by a family, with a private residence adjacent to the military camp.

In a legion the highest-ranking officer was the *praefectus castrorum* (camp prefect), and this was open to centurions. Centurions aspired to lead a 480-man cohort and become its "first centurion" or *primus pilus* (first spear), leading the "first cohort." Nevertheless the centurion always "belonged" to his century—an infantry force of eighty men under his direct command. The centurions were Roman citizens and were well paid, often ten times the pay of regular troops (about 5,000 denarii per year). Their loyalty to the emperor was unmatched, and they were well-known for the oaths they took not only to the legionnaire's life but to the success of Rome itself.

Centurions trained their legionary soldiers, fought alongside them, distributed honors, and prosecuted discipline. They could even exact the death penalty. The late fourth-century writer Vegetius (Flavius Vegetius Renatus) wrote a Latin book entitled *Concerning Military Matters* (*De re militari*) in which he described the role of the centurion. The treatise was later used for over 1,300 years as a guide to military organization:

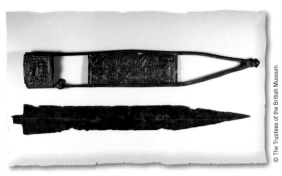

A TYPICAL ROMAN SWORD FOUND AMONG THE LEGIONS.

A SHIELD TYPICAL OF THOSE USED BY ROMAN IMPERIAL LEGIONS.

A FIBULA, THE CLASP FOR A CENTURION'S CLOAK.

Every century has its ensign and every troop its standard. The centurion in the infantry is chosen for his size, strength and dexterity in throwing his missile weapons and for his skill in the use of his sword and shield; in short for his expertise in all the exercises. He is to be vigilant, temperate, active and readier to execute the orders he receives than to talk; strict in exercising and keeping up proper discipline among his soldiers, in obliging them to appear clean and well-dressed and to have their arms constantly polished and bright.[5]

It should come as no surprise that centurions appear in the gospel story. Centurions supervised both Jesus' crucifixion (Mark 15:44) and the guarding of his tomb (Matt. 27:54). If a Jew in Judea ever had contact with the army, a centurion was likely nearby. Because Capernaum was not only a tax station in Galilee but also stood on a strategic road, Roman infantry were stationed there. Centurions in such villages had remarkable authority. They could confiscate property for "official" use (possibly Luke 6:29), they could force labor from the population (Matt. 5:41), and in one case, a centurion ordered a man named Simon from Cyrene to carry Jesus' cross (27:32). They enforced taxation and suppressed unrest and in many cases were brutal. For all these reasons they were hated by the population. The Roman infantry implemented the conquest and occupation of their country.

On the ground level, the centurions made the day-to-day decisions during local crises. They represented blunt authority of Rome to the average person.

CAPERNAUM'S CENTURION

We learn about Capernaum's centurion in one story that is recorded in both Matthew and Luke (Matthew 8:5–13; Luke 7:1–10). To the average Jewish reader in antiquity, such a story would have been astonishing. You did not *befriend* centurions; you *avoided* centurions.

What can we know about this man? We can assume that he was deeply loyal to Rome and already had demonstrated many years of military service. If he was serving with his century (and we have no reason to think otherwise), he was in command of eighty men in Capernaum who had a military camp outside town. The centurion had almost absolute control over his designated region and could not be challenged. He could arrest anyone, and his decisions affecting the local population were rarely questioned. We can also assume he was moderately wealthy and lived in one of the town's nicest villas somewhere on the perimeter of the village, possibly just to the east.[16]

The centurion was also influential and well-known in Capernaum. The elders of the village knew him by name and worked closely with him. But among many he was both feared and hated. Extremists wanted him killed. The elders, for whom purity was important, avoided him since he was a Gentile and *unclean*. Coming to his headquarters always ended with a ritual bath for ritual cleansing.[17] This meant he lived primarily with his troops, moving like a satellite around Capernaum's periphery, watching the conduct of its residents carefully. We also know that Jesus lived here, and we should assume that Jesus knew exactly who he was.

THE REQUEST

This particular man for whom authority and control were everything has a problem he cannot control. One of his slaves is critically ill, near death, and he does not know what to do. Every legion had medical staff, but here he is separated from them, and he is left to rely on whatever local resources are available.

His concern about a slave is the first window we have into this man. It is hard for us today to imagine the social status of a slave in the Roman Empire. Slaves were everywhere and had numerous classifications. Some families sold children into slavery. Some sold themselves as a result of debt. In the urban centers, the slave population could reach 30 percent. In the rural areas, it was 15 to 20 percent. But conquest was a chief source for

AN IVORY CARVING OF A DISFIGURED SLAVE FROM THE ROMAN PERIOD.

CAPERNAUM SYNAGOGUE SHOWING THE WHITE WALLS
AND BLACK BASALT ON THE LOWER LEVEL.

slaves. Professional slavers would follow the army and pur-
chase the conquered, later selling them for profit. After his
successful campaign in Gaul (58–51 BC), Julius Caesar once
emptied an entire district and enslaved all 53,000 of its people,
selling them to slavers.[18]

Even though slaves were counted as "family" among the
Romans, they were cheap. They cost about one week's wage for
a centurion. They rarely had medical care and had a life expec-
tancy of less than thirty years. But this centurion is concerned
about one slave, and it is striking that he is so worried. Does
he *value* this slave? Does he know this slave personally? Does
he have a relationship with him? Does this centurion have a
disposition toward people we would not expect?

The second window into this centurion's life is his relationship with the Jewish community of Capernaum. The elders
report to Jesus that the centurion "loves our people" and moreover, he built the Capernaum synagogue (Luke 7:5). This is
remarkable behavior. It would be cynical to conclude that this
project is merely an investment to control the town by winning
the synagogue elders. He understands the Jewish community
and respects it. In other words, the centurion has become a
civic benefactor of Capernaum. In Roman cities, leading citizens
would enhance their honor by providing public buildings for

the enjoyment of all. In city after city, century after century, Roman public buildings can be found with inscriptions listing the honored benefactors who built them.[19] This centurion is behaving with affection toward Capernaum as if he were in his own home city somewhere in the Roman Empire.

A man in his position—if he knew that a famous healer had arrived in his precinct—might send a courier and order him to come to his home. This was the nature of his world. And this particular centurion admits it. "I tell this one, 'Go,' and he goes; and that one, 'Come,' and he comes" (Luke 7:8). But this is not what he himself does. He understands that he is a Gentile, he understands the boundaries imposed on him by Jewish law, and he recognizes that he cannot demand a righteous Jewish teacher and healer to enter his villa. His solution is not to send a few of his legionnaires; rather, his solution is to ask a favor from the Jewish elders. He has been the patron of the Jewish community, helping it where needed, and now he comes to ask a favor. *Would they go as a delegation to Jesus?*

And this is what the elders do. Alone they plead with Jesus to take care of the centurion's needs. Some have suggested that this was an obligatory duty they sensed from their benefactor, the man who built their synagogue. But this view is not necessary. The centurion is not one of their own; he is not a

THIS INSCRIPTION FOUND IN CORINTH LISTS BABBIUS AS A BENEFACTOR OF THE CITY.

citizen of Capernaum. Their sense of duty to him is limited. So there must be another motivation. Is it possible that they like this man? That they respect him? That his concern has now become theirs? Is the centurion a "God-fearer" like Cornelius (Acts 10:2), a man who believes in the God of Israel and yet has taken no public steps toward conversion? The centurion's dependency on the elders is also something that puts him at risk with his own troops. Instead of commanding obedience, he may be showing weakness and vulnerability. *Compassion* was not a frequent word in the vocabulary of legionary infantry.

THE ENCOUNTER

Other encounter stories remind us that village life was a very public affair lived for the most part outside. Matters of even trivial news were discussed daily at length. These transactions between the elders and the centurion—as well as Jesus and the elders—did not take place privately. News of Jesus' arrival sweeps through the village. Audiences who have heard him earlier likely follow him again. When the elders approach Jesus with their request, already a crowd has formed (Luke 7:9). And an array of questions is present: Will Jesus deny the request of elders he knows well? Will he refuse the needs of the most

A SEVENTEENTH-CENTURY PAINTING BY SEBASTIEN BOURDON (1616–1671) DEPICTS CHRIST WITH THE CENTURION AND THE ELDERS.

Christ and the Centurion, Bourdon, Sebastien/Musee des Beaux-Arts, Caen, France/Giraudon/The Bridgeman Art Library

ENCOUNTERS WITH JESUS

www.BigStockPhoto.com

THE ROMAN AQUEDUCT AT CAESAREA MARITIMA EXHIBITS THE IMPRESSIVE ARCHITECTURAL ACHIEVEMENTS OF ROME IN JUDEA.

powerful Roman in the region and jeopardize the good relationship the village has with him?

Jesus agrees to come and help. And as he walks toward the centurion's home, yet another surprising development shifts the story. Surely the crowd is amazed at the prospect of Jesus' coming to see the centurion. A righteous man such as Jesus would hardly enter a Gentile's home. Plus there might be surprises when he arrives there: perhaps idols, concubines, and no doubt food prohibited to Jews. Surely the village drama heightens — surely the crowd begins to swell — as Jesus walks with the elders, followed by a crowd, toward the Roman military camp.

As they near the house, the group is stopped short. A good friend of the centurion — a Roman, no doubt — brings a message from the centurion himself: "Lord, don't trouble yourself, for I do not deserve to have you come under my roof. That is why I did not even consider myself worthy to come to you. But say the word, and my servant will be healed" (Luke 7:6 – 7). The centurion is doing something here that is important: *he is respecting a religious boundary.* First-century Judaism was a boundary-legislating culture that marked off the limits of righteous behavior carefully. Gender boundaries were common, limiting male-female contact. Health boundaries likewise isolated any with

A SILVER COIN WITH A BUST
OF TIBERIUS CAESAR,
EMPEROR DURING
JESUS' LIFETIME.

visible disease. And here ethnic boundaries were in play. A well-informed Roman understood the self-imposed boundaries Judaism placed on itself just as a Gentile would today if he or she were hosting orthodox Jews. This centurion is willing to concede and adopt the Jewish perspective. In his mind, Jesus would not want to enter his home.

Suddenly the centurion presents himself not as a commander, but as a suppliant. He has taken a weaker position, asking for what he can and leaving Jesus to preserve his own religious status.

The centurion's words also unveil another surprising perspective. He sees in Jesus' life something that paralleled his own career. He is a man who knows how to give orders. *He has authority.* The courier's message continues, "For I myself am a man under authority, with soldiers under me. I tell this one, 'Go,' and he goes; and that one, 'Come,' and he comes. I say to my servant, 'Do this,' and he does it" (7:8). The basis of the centurion's confidence in Jesus stems from his own instinctive knowledge about power, and he intuits that Jesus has that power.

Imbedded in this perspective is a tacit assumption about the origins of Jesus' authority. In the centurion's world, his power stems entirely from the imperial legions that stand behind him. And ultimately that power rested with Tiberius Caesar in Rome, who could command every legion to march. The centurion understands that Jesus is similarly empowered by God in a way that others are not. He too belongs to a kingdom, and that kingdom likewise has power.

We must imagine this scene for all of its drama. Both Jesus and the centurion may have been in the street, separated by a delegation of Jewish elders and a crowd. Perhaps they can see each other. Despite the gulf that separates them, Jesus is willing to cross it; yet, out of deference and respect, the centurion declines. "But say the word, and my servant will be healed" (Luke 7:7) are the words of one commander giving a recommendation to another.

There are only two times in the Gospels where it says

A painting by James Tissot (1836–1902) shows the centurion turning down Jesus' offer to visit his home.

that Jesus was astonished (Gk. *thaumazô*), here and in Mark 6:6. Before the entire Jewish crowd, Jesus holds up the centurion as a model of faith. "I tell you, I have not found such great faith even in Israel" (Luke 7:9). It is here that Matthew provides more detail by recording Jesus' fuller response.

> *I say to you that many will come from the east and the west, and will take their places at the feast with Abraham, Isaac and Jacob in the kingdom of heaven. But the subjects of the kingdom will be thrown outside, into the darkness, where there will be weeping and gnashing of teeth.* (Matt. 8:11–12)

Abraham's fellowship was the goal of all faithful Jews. And here Jesus provides an answer that will be echoed by Paul (Rom. 4; Gal. 3) and Luke (Acts 11:18). In popular Jewish thought it was agreed that many Jews might not be worthy to join Abraham at the great messianic banquet at the end of

THE MOSAIC DINING ROOM FLOOR OF A
ROMAN VILLA IN SEPPHORIS, GALILEE.

time, but at least it would be a Jewish feast. Here Jesus amends this view. A Gentile such as this centurion could be identified with the family of Abraham—as will be many others outside Israel ("east and west")—while those who count on ethnic religious privileges may find themselves at a loss. These are symbolized elsewhere in Jesus' parables as the disobedient son (Matt. 21:28–32), the defaulting tenants (21:33–44), and those who reject their invitation to the feast (21:1–10).[20]

FAITH AND THE CENTURION

If Jesus was taking social risks in his overture to Zacchaeus the tax collector (chapter 3), he has now gone further. He has ignored boundaries that separate "the Gentile" and applauded faith where he finds it no matter the ethnic or religious background. Every culture is quick to identify who the "Gentiles" are. Jesus will have none of it.

But it is the profile of the centurion that genuinely stands out. He is a man who understands authority. He also understands subordination and obedience. Therefore he instinctively understands the mechanics of faith in a way that few others might grasp. He "encounters" Jesus to be sure; but more, Jesus "encounters" him and admires what he sees.

But within this man's life, those native reflexes that have

made him what he is—a leading military officer—have been refined and changed. Here we see a courageous man with courageous humility. No arrogance. Like Zacchaeus, he is not a bad man who needs conversion. He was a good man who is being discovered.

Among the many "encounter stories" of the New Testament, this is perhaps one of the most remarkable. We have seen two stories thus far that showcase the unique features of their main character. The woman with the hemorrhage of blood (chapter 2) surfaces in the story as a woman of remarkable boldness and courage, risking all to encounter Jesus. Zacchaeus of Jericho (chapter 3) appears as a man of wealth and power for whom surprising generosity and honesty are hallmarks. In each story, some feature of the person's life is engaged and highlighted. An unclean woman touches Jesus. An ostracized tax collector is discovered to be a benefactor for the poor. These are unexpected things whose surprises are embedded in the culture of their world.

The account of the centurion of Capernaum is like these. And it centers on a man of significant military prowess for whom power is intrinsic to who he is. Without authority the centurion knows he is useless as a military leader. Yet some transformation is afoot. His approach is noticeably different. Faith has been at work. And Jesus sees it and celebrates it publicly.

Chapter 5

A Woman in Samaria

John 4:4–26

IN EACH of the "encounters" we have studied thus far, a pattern has emerged. Some feature of the person's life, some signature trait, has surfaced in their encounter with Jesus. It may have been their personality, their job, their circumstances—it really does not matter. But in the encounter with Jesus, a fundamental element of who they were was engaged. And in many cases it was transformed.

The woman with the hemorrhage of blood was *defined* no doubt by her circumstances and desperation. The arrival of Jesus provoked in her boldness and determination that even shocked her village. Jesus was impressed by this. Zacchaeus of Jericho was a skilled investor on whom the town had heaped many stereotypes. Yet here we find a man for whom money was a tool, but it did not define him. He was profoundly generous and honest. This impressed Jesus too. The centurion of Capernaum was a man defined by power. Yet his encounter with Jesus unmasked his true relationship to power and authority. He held it loosely.

Each of these stories invites us to wonder what it would mean if we encountered Jesus in such a manner. What defining

THE ROMAN THEATER IN SAMARIA.

characteristics of our lives would surface? What essential features would get unmasked? What things would he admire? What would change?

One of the most dramatic "encounter" stories in the Gospels is found in John 4. Jesus is traveling north from Jerusalem to Galilee. And when he passes through a region called Samaria, he encounters a remarkable woman.

Samaria

From an ancient Jewish perspective, Samaria was notorious and ought to be avoided. Samaria was a region in Israel's central mountains directly north of Jerusalem. If a person was traveling north from Jerusalem to Galilee, the route through Samaria was easier, but it forced the traveler to enter this

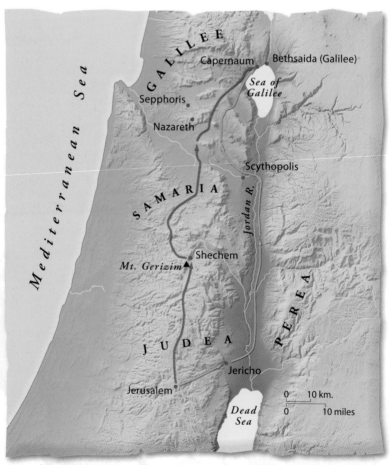

ROUTES THROUGH AND AROUND SAMARIA.

LOOKING ACROSS THE JEZREEL VALLEY TO
MT. GILBOA—A LANDMARK FOR ANCIENT TRAVELERS.

region inhabited by people with whom rivalry and strife had
an ancient history.[21] The usual route took you east. Travelers
would go east to Jericho and then travel north, skirting the
hills of Judea and Samaria with the Jordan River basin on their
right side. When Mount Gilboa came into view, they came to
the Greek city of Scythopolis (Old Testament Beth Shan) and
turned in (west) to the Jezreel Valley, whose open, well-watered
plains guided them into Galilee's interior.

In Jesus' day Jews viewed Samaritans with skepticism
and prejudice. After the reign of Solomon, ancient Israel was
split in two: the north (Samaria) and the south (anchored at

THE OPEN PLAINS OF THE JEZREEL VALLEY.

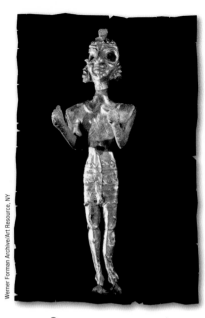

SAMARITAN HISTORY WAS WELL KNOWN FOR IDOLATRY. HERE IS A CANAANITE GOLD AND SILVER BRONZE FIGURE OF BAAL.

Jerusalem). Jews in Jesus' day remembered the ancient stories of the apostasy of the northern kingdom that was based here. This was the world of Ahab and Jezebel, two of Israel's most notorious leaders. Then in 722 BC, a foreign army (the Assyrians) conquered Samaria, exiled many of its residents, and repopulated the area with other people from throughout its empire (2 Kings 17:23–24). Remnants of the old defeated northern Israelite kingdom were soon mixed with Persians and other conquered peoples. The paganism known to the Israelite king Jeroboam was blended with countless other practices, making the religious impurity of the land infamous (17:25–41).

In time, belief in the one God of Israel won the day, but this faith suffered important changes. The Samaritans rejected the writings of the prophets (including the histories [Kings, Chronicles]) and the wisdom literature (Proverbs, Psalms, etc.) because these writings emphasized the southern lands of Judea and David's rule centered on Jerusalem. Their scriptures were limited to the first five books of the Bible (Genesis through Deuteronomy), and their worship was organized around a new temple on Mount Gerizim, towering above ancient Shechem. They repudiated Jerusalem as a place of worship and pilgrimage.

Relationships between the Jews in Jerusalem and the Samaritans were always tense. After the Babylonians destroyed Jerusalem (586 BC), many Jews returned, and Ezra led the rebuilding of the Jerusalem temple. The Samaritans sought an alliance with Ezra and offered to help restore Jerusalem. But the offer was rejected (Ezra 4), and this only added to the tensions.

When Alexander the Great and later Greek generals conquered Palestine (from about 330 BC), they made Samaria an important base, knowing that here they could find sympathetic, anti-Jewish allies. When the Jews of Jerusalem had their opportunity (128 BC), they attacked Samaria, destroyed Shechem, and burned the Samaritan temple on Mount Gerizim. During a time of political turmoil (AD 6) the Samaritans returned the favor one Passover by cleverly sneaking into the Jerusalem temple at midnight with hidden bags of human bones from a cemetery. Then

THE RUINS OF SHECHEM
WITH MT. GERIZIM IN THE
BACKGROUND

they threw them all around the temple courtyards and made the building "unclean" and unusable for worship.[22]

By Jesus' day, a smoldering tension existed between the regions of Judea and Samaria. Partly based on race and religion, it echoed many centuries of terrible political fights. This underscores the shock of Jesus' parable about the good Samaritan (Luke 10:35–37). In it Jesus made an enemy a hero.

Therefore, when we read in John 4 that Jesus passes through the region of Samaria and meets a "Samaritan woman," immediately our cultural antennae should go up. *This is irregular.* Here is a woman bearing the history, language, religion, and attitudes of people on the far margin of

THE ROMAN FORUM AND ITS
COLUMNS IN SAMARIA ARE
FROM THE TIME OF ALEXANDER
THE GREAT.

THE OLD TESTAMENT CITY GATE AT ANCIENT SHECHEM.

Judaism. Anyone who first heard this story in Jesus' day would barely expect Jesus and the woman to acknowledge each other, much less speak. Their worlds did not mingle.

The story says that they meet at a place called "Sychar" (John 4:5). The problem is that no such place exists in any of our records. A modern Arab village has a similar name ('Askar), but it is only a thousand years old. Likely the location is ancient Shechem (Gen. 33:19; 48:22). Even though there is no biblical record of Jacob digging a well here, it is not unlikely, and today an ancient well is accessible adjacent to Shechem. It is probably best to conclude that Sychar refers then to Shechem, and the well nearby that city is the historic well.

BOUNDARIES

Jesus lived in a world of strict social boundaries. This was reinforced by a preoccupation with rules for purity that registered what was permitted or prohibited. The differences with our world could not be more stark. Recently I met a female friend for lunch. We were alone, in an expensive restaurant, unaccompanied by our spouses. When we greeted each other, we hugged. And that afternoon I thought about how cultural values in our world have given us permission in a manner unknown two thousand years ago. In Jesus' day, that lunch meeting would have never happened. Our society has gender boundaries, but they are far different than what was enforced in Jewish antiquity. To get a sense of a firm "racial" and "gender" boundary in operation, we'd have to return to a southern city like Birmingham in the 1950s. And there we could imagine a same-age young black man and a young white woman alone in a restaurant at night. That society once had strict (and tragic) prohibitions that were widely known.

In the world of the Gospels, boundaries that prohibited contact or behavior served to protect honor and social status. In some cases — as in rules that controlled how unmarried men and women could meet — they protected the purity of families and moral values, and they avoided the possibility of unfortunate accusations.

When Jesus meets the Samaritan woman, numerous boundaries are violated. This explains the disciples' astonishment when they see him there. "Just then his disciples returned and were surprised to find him talking with a woman. But no one asked, 'What do you want?' or 'Why are you talking with her?' " (John 4:27). This passage is actually being discreet. If we read between the lines, *they are shocked that Jesus is talking to a*

A WOMAN IN NINETEENTH-CENTURY
PALESTINE POSES FOR A PHOTO REMINISCENT
OF WATERDRAWING IN ANTIQUITY.

woman, but they do not want to ask what he is doing. They sense the irregularity. Their minds are racing with thoughts they dare not express: "What was going on here? Why this irregular conversation?" The surprising thing is not that Jesus has asked her for help with a drink of water. It is that he would ask her *anything.* The disciples are reluctant to point out something (in their minds) Jesus surely should have known.

What boundaries set off alarms? Private social contact between men and women unmarried to one another was restricted in that world. This was a world of arranged marriages, where "social dating" was unknown. In fact, in this world men rarely spoke to women in public, particularly if they were not from their family (or kinship group). And single (unattached) men never spoke to or touched nonfamily women. Above all, a rabbi (as Jesus is known) would have observed these ideals scrupulously. This explains the woman's surprise in 4:9: she is not merely a Samaritan, but a Samaritan *woman.*

But there is also a cultural/ethnic tension. She is a Samaritan and Jesus is a Jew. Their clothing and dialects certainly give them away. And as the story unfolds, we learn that she is a woman with an illicit reputation, and of course Jesus is a righteous man. They are therefore opposites: male/female, Jew/Gentile, righteous/unrighteous. *They should have no contact.*

THE WELL

When Jesus comes to Samaria and approaches Jacob's well, it is about noon. And this is where he meets the woman. The *location* of their meeting now enhances the irregularity of the moment. First, in this culture water collection was the responsibility of women. (This explains why in Mark 14:13 Jesus can use a man carrying water as a signal for his disciples to locate the room of his final Passover. It was the perfect disguise.)

In a world that isolated women socially, the task was not entirely burdensome but became an opportunity for women to meet and talk. Therefore wells became the one preserve, the one locale where women could be either avoided (or met). When Abraham's servant returned north to Haran looking for a wife for Isaac, he found the local well (Gen. 24) and there met Rebekah. He knew where to find the women. Likewise, Moses fled to Midian and at a well met the daughters of Jethro (Ex. 2:15–16), one of whom becomes his wife (Zipporah).

Library of Congress, LC-DIG-matpc-06484

JACOB'S WELL IN SHECHEM.

I remember once traveling in the rural West Bank with a British ambulance team. We were in a village not far from Nablus (near Shechem), and while our team set up the clinic, I decided (naively) to go looking for the village's ancient well. The well had been covered with a modest stone building, which (as I was about to learn) was the private domain of the women. As I approached, two things happened: the men of the village began walking speedily in my direction from the fields. Then the ambulance driver sprinted my way (with arms waving wildly) to escort me out of there. The women used the building to hang and dry their lingerie *since of course no men ever entered.* And young women were in there doing things that no man should (apparently) see. Simply put, there was (and is) an intimate connotation linked to wells. Moses was lucky. Jethro's daughters enjoyed his visit—and he married one of them.

This motif is so prominent that some scholars have suggested that something more is going on in this story. If Jesus is alone at a well with a woman, are there echoes of an ancient betrothal scene? A man alone with a woman is a classic ancient scene for romance. And as we learn eventually, this is a woman who has suffered greatly with failed love throughout her past. But here she will discover a new redeeming relationship with a man who will offer her what she least expects.[23]

In the first century, the well itself would have had a short perimeter wall around its mouth (preventing people, animals,

A TYPICAL WELL, INCLUDING A STONE TROUGH NEARBY FOR ANIMALS TO BE WATERED.

and debris from falling in), a stone lid (see Gen. 29:2), a stone trough nearby for animals to be watered, and perhaps a tripod for attaching a rope and a container for drawing water. Jesus arrives at the well, sits on the wall at the well's edge to relieve his fatigue, and presents an unavoidable obstacle to a woman who has come to get water.[24]

THE ENCOUNTER

The Jewish pattern was to count the hours of the day from sunrise (Romans, like us, counted from midnight). The "sixth hour," then, refers to noon. But at once we meet another irregularity. Women collected water at sunrise and dusk — not in the middle of the day. Therefore this woman is alone, isolated for some reason from her community.

We have to imagine the scene: the woman arrives at the famed well with a water jar; Jesus sits on its lid or edge, and he poses an obvious problem. We can excuse the woman for wondering what he was up to. *She had known wayward men.* Here is one on the road alone. And she too is alone. *What does he really want?* Jesus' initial question ("Will you give me a drink?") seemed innocent enough, but it deserves a rebuff. "You are a Jew and I am a Samaritan woman. How can you ask me for a drink?" (John 4:9). She is establishing the boundaries. A gentle reminder of their respective "places" might make this situation go away.

Jesus then does something remarkable. *He offers her a drink.* They are playing cultural tennis—positioning themselves delicately, exchanging overtures, watching for nuance. How can he offer something like this? He has no tools to use at the well, no rope or vessel. But he says more: that if she knew the gift of God in front of her and asked, he could supply *living water.*

Suddenly, these words shift everything. I can imagine the woman taking a step back. She will either fight or flee; her muscles would tense at the reference.

A HELLENISTIC WOMAN FROM THE ROMAN PERIOD WEARING CONTEMPORARY MODEST ATTIRE.

It is impossible to understand what happens next without exploring this term. Judaism carefully distinguished "living water" from other water. It had nothing to do with the quality or taste of the water. It was a ritual tool. "Living water" referred to water that flowed as in a spring, river, or stream. It might be a lake. It was water that had not been elevated or moved by human hand but had come directly from the hand of God. And because it came directly from God, it had unique heavenly properties. Living water was

CHRIST OFFERS THE WOMAN LIVING WATER IN A PAINTING BY CARLO MARATTA (1625–1713).

precious and valued and according to rabbinic law, it was the *only* water that could be used in ritual washings to make pure unclean worshipers. It was so powerful that a single drop of living water was capable of making an entire ritual bath potent. For example, if a pond formed by rainfall were in a village, the water would be "clean." But if a Gentile were to touch it (or a dead body fall into it), the water became "unclean." If it rained some more—just a drop—the law understood that this rain, directly from God, could make the pool clean once again.[25]

Therefore Jesus suggests that he knows where such unique water can be found. Yet this is remarkable. Everyone knew that Shechem had no rivers or streams. Even Jacob had to dig a well in order to water his flocks here (John 4:12). How could a Jewish outsider, someone who barely knew the terrain, offer water that no one else had found? There is no convenient living water in Shechem unless it had been captured by rainfall.

Yet Jesus wonders two things. Will the woman recognize that she is being confronted with a remarkable opportunity (a gift, John 4:10), and will she take the risk of asking for this water? For a second time, she tries to rebuff him. "Are you greater than our father Jacob, who gave us the well and drank from it himself, as did also his sons and his flocks and herds" (4:12)? *Of course he is!* But Jesus continues to explain, expounding on what living water can actually do. It can remove thirst permanently—and create a spring in a person's heart—and lead to eternal life.

Then, at last, the woman takes the risk Jesus hoped to see, "Sir, give me this water so that I won't get thirsty and have to keep coming here to draw water" (John 4:15).

A RITUAL BATH (OR MIKVEH) FROM QUMRAN THAT USED LIVING WATER FOR CEREMONIAL CLEANSING.

The Woman's Courage

The woman's request for water, for living water, is not about convenience. Nor is it about her pottery vessel and the water she can take home in it. *It is about cleansing—and restoration.* Jesus is provoking her to think about a sort of water that will restore her to a place with God that she has not known for years. To offer a stranger a drink of water might be a gesture of hospitality and friendship. To suggest she needs living water is something different; it is prophetic.

Immediately after the woman requests this water, Jesus probes further. "Go, call your husband and come back" (John 4:16). But she denies that she has a husband. So Jesus continues, "You are right when you say you have no husband. The fact is, you have had five husbands, and the man you now have is not your husband" (4:17–18). In Jewish law, a woman could not divorce her husband, so she may well have been the victim of unscrupulous men who had dismissed her. But this woman knows that Jesus has unmasked something important. *He is probing near the very thing that defines her.* She is now in an immoral relationship (did this suggest other habits?). And these words from Jesus have a divine mark on them (4:19).

Then for the third time she rebuffs him. She throws up the very item that has separated Jews and Samaritans for centuries. "Our ancestors worshiped on this mountain, but you Jews claim that the place where we must worship is in Jerusalem" (John 4:20). The Samaritans had a temple built on Mount Gerizim near

The landscape of Shechem.

THE VIEW OF SAMARIA FROM THE TOP OF MT. GERIZIM.

Shechem, and its rival was the temple of Jerusalem. She again is asserting boundaries, wondering if this man will retreat, if he will concede the ancient divisions and withdraw. Today she might have said, "Look, you're a Yankee Catholic from Boston, and I'm a Southern Baptist from Atlanta. Need I say more?"

And with a sentence Jesus demolishes the ancient boundary. Mount Gerizim and Jerusalem are not important; the only question is whether or not a person has encountered the Spirit of God (John 4:21–22). Because God is Spirit—he is neither Jew nor Samaritan—to worship him transformed by *his Spirit* is to worship in truth (4:24). Ethnic boundaries and religious markers are impediments to discovering this God.

The woman's last comment was her final attempt to push this man away. And from here, her defenses crumble. She makes her first genuine spiritual overture: she believes in the Messiah! She looks with longing for his coming! She believes that he will reveal everything! Then Jesus unveils the gift he has promised from the beginning: I am he (John 4:26).

FAITH AND THE SAMARITAN WOMAN

I am constantly impressed with this woman. Here is a woman who has a dozen reasons to disqualify herself. She knows that she has been living in isolation not only from her community but from God. And her brokenness is continually before her eyes. Yet as her conversation with Jesus deepens, *she does not flee.* She remains in this awkward relationship and does not shut down. When she hears what Jesus has to say about her private history, she does not fight it but silently acknowledges that living water is precisely what she yearns for. She yearns for the ritual bath, the mikveh, that will change everything—to begin again, to be forgiven, to see herself as clean and pure and renewed in a way that she once thought impossible.

In the end, she recognizes that she doesn't really want well water. Thus, in a gesture that is at once forgetful and symbolic, she leaves her jar behind at the well (John 4:28) and sprints into her village to tell the people from whom she has been estranged that perhaps —just perhaps—she has found the Messiah.

A JAR REPRESENTING THE TYPE OF POTTERY THAT A WOMAN WOULD HAVE USED TO CARRY WATER FROM THE WELL.

www.ancienttouch.com

The profile of Jesus in this encounter is also intriguing. In Samaria he has taken a risk. Of course, for a Jew to be in Samaria was risky enough. But here he is willing to meet alone at a well with a woman possessing a "reputation," a woman who is a social outcast. But this does not concern him. He sees a harvest that is ripe among people like this, and he is fully and completely committed to them (John 4:34–38).

But the woman is not just one more convert. He is interested in her. He knows the details of her life. He is awkwardly persistent and willing to become an obstacle. He never gets up from the well that she wants to use. Moreover, he is willing to raise the hard questions to move her to a place of life and hope.

In an encounter story like this one, we see the patience of Jesus meeting the courage of a forgotten woman. And the most profound need of her life—restoration—is the one gift that Jesus has offered her.

Chapter 6

A GREEK WOMAN IN TYRE

Matthew 15:21–28; Mark 7:24–30

THROUGHOUT THE Gospels, stories tell us again and again about the boldness of people who encounter Jesus. We saw this initially in the story of the hemorrhaging woman (chapter 2). Here was a woman living in extreme social isolation who believed that her one chance at healing had arrived with Jesus. She moved through the crowd with determination, and when she was close enough, she grabbed the hem of Jesus' garment. She stopped the entire parade and surely outraged the village elders. She is an exemplar of faith whose story is preserved because it models something important for every reader of the Gospels.

Stories about boldness abound in our Gospels. But the oddest story—and certainly the shortest—is found in Matthew 15 and Mark 7. It is the only time we learn about Jesus leaving the province of Judea and ministering directly to a Gentile. A Greek woman with a desperately ill daughter knows of his reputation. And she comes to him and asks for her daughter to be healed. The conversation that evolves between them is one of the most famous in the Gospels.

The Region of Tyre

When Rome conquered the eastern Mediterranean, it organized these regions into provinces. In some cases, easily pacified regions might answer directly to administrative councils of the Roman Senate. In cases where a province was volatile or strategically valuable, a large detachment of soldiers — organized in "legions" — was posted and worked directly with the emperor and his military advisors.

Jesus belonged to the Roman province of Judea, named thus for the Jews (Gk. *Ioudaioi*, Judeans) who lived there; they also lived in the local region of Galilee. Judea was a small province centered around Jerusalem. Its boundary included southern deserts around Old Testament Beersheba, the hills east of the Dead Sea and Jordan River (called Perea), the high plateau in the northeast (today's Golan Heights), on the north the mountainous terrain south of Mount Hermon, and the entire area of Galilee. From an ancient Jewish worldview, the Romans had

TYRE AND SURROUNDING AREA.

stitched together Judea, Samaria, Perea, Galilee, and the northeast deserts. The province was bounded on the south and southeast by the Arab kingdom of Nabatea. On the north, it met the powerful Roman province of Syria, where Rome stationed at least one legion.

AERIAL PHOTO OF TYRE AND ITS CAUSEWAY CONNECTION TO THE COAST.

DigitalGlobe/Getty Images

Syria was huge and served as a buttress against any advances of the Persian army in the east. It blocked the mighty Euphrates River and controlled trade from its chief city of Antioch on the Orontes River. Its outline in the south followed the modern coast of Lebanon and took in important trading cities we would recognize today: Berytus (modern Beirut), Sidon, and Tyre. These were Greek regions; they were wealthy and devoted to imperial ambitions in the east. Of course they knew their neighbors to the south, but they would have seen Judea as provincial, small, and no doubt quaint. It wasn't until the reign of Herod the Great (37–4 BC) that suddenly Judea began to get noticed.

Tyre was Syria's southernmost coastal city. The region around it (from Berytus to Tyre) also went by its ancient name — Phoenicia — harking back to the ancient seafaring people who lived there. To call it "Syria-Phoenicia" would have been common. Tyre began as an offshore island whose wealth and significance are attested throughout the Old Testament. King David's conquest of the Philistine army helped Tyre defeat the Philistine navy and so control more trade. Tyre's king Hiram I (969–936 BC) thanked David by sending cedar and workmen to build David's palace (2 Sam. 5:11). Even

Solomon used artisans from Tyre to help adorn the new temple he built in Jerusalem (1 Kings 5:16–20).

A large city on the mainland expanded Tyre. The metropolis became a major commercial trade center and was famous (among other things) for its trade in purple dye harvested from the murex snail shell found nearby. This dye was so famous that imperial coins from Tyre even printed the snail as a city emblem.

When Alexander the Great conquered Tyre (332 BC), he destroyed the mainland city and used the rubble to build a causeway out to the island; it was a half mile long and about 250 yards wide. After a seven-month siege, using both infantry and naval bombardment, Tyre was defeated. Four hundred of Alexander's troops died, but thousands of Tyrians lost their lives. He crucified 2,000 prisoners, sold 30,000 of its citizens into slavery, and began building a strategic port for his empire immediately.[26] Within a hundred years Tyre had regained its stature.

The province of Judea always sought Tyre's favor. This was a city of prestige and a well-connected port to the Mediterranean world. As ships circled

A COIN FROM TYRE—THE ONLY COIN ACCEPTED BY THE JERUSALEM TEMPLE—HERE SHOWS THE MUREX SHELL ON ITS REVERSE SIDE.

SHELLS OF MUREX SNAILS, WHICH WERE USED TO MAKE PURPLE DYE.

Beast Coins

Z. Radovan/www.BibleLandPictures.com

the Mediterranean following routes to Egypt, Tyre was a waypoint. Its markets and temples were monolithic. It had the largest horse racing track (or hippodrome) in the entire Roman Empire and a main columned street that was 550 feet long and 36 feet wide. It was well-known for its devotion to the god Heracles. Herod the Great visited Tyre regularly (Josephus, *Jewish War* 1.231–38, 275, 543) and contributed columned markets and temples for the city (*Jewish War* 1.422).

RUINS IN THE ANCIENT CITY OF TYRE.

Trade between Tyre and Judea was common. Coins from Tyre have turned up in excavations throughout Galilee, and its pure silver coins (complete with an eagle on one side, and on the reverse, an image of Melqart, the deity of Tyre) were required to pay the half-shekel annual tax at the temple (Mishnah, *Shekalim* 1:1–3). A later Jewish saying tells us, "Silver mentioned in the Five Books of Moses is always Tyrian silver: What is Tyrian silver? It is Jerusalemite" (Tosefta, *Ketubot* 13:20). In 1955 archaeologists at Qumran near the Dead

THE REMAINS OF THE TYRE HIPPODROME.

Sea discovered a buried jar holding over five hundred silver coins — most of them from Tyre.[27] In 2008 one such coin was discovered in the excavation of a drainage channel just south of Jerusalem's walled city, today called the City of David. These are rare and only about a half dozen have been discovered by archaeologists in the city. But these discoveries point to the use of the coins in Jewish life during Jesus' day.

JESUS AND GENTILES

Jesus restricted the work of his disciples to the Jews. He even limited the range of their movement to the province of Judea. We have no record of Jesus telling them to go to Egypt or even to nearby Syria (although they did cross over to the other side of the Jordan, Mark 10:1; John 10:40). On one occasion he told them, "Do not go among the Gentiles or enter any town of the Samaritans. Go rather to the lost sheep of Israel" (Matt. 10:5–6). This has resulted in considerable controversy among scholars about Jesus' ethnic exclusivity. Did he really care anything about Gentiles? Did he believe in a "Gentile mission"?[28]

The exclusivity of Judaism — separating it from the Gentile world — is well-known. But there is evidence in the Gospels that Jesus was already promoting something broader. The first hint is in his genealogy, where three non-Jews are listed (Matt. 1:3–6, see Tamar and Rahab, both Canaanites; and Ruth, a Moabite).

We know too that Jesus was willing to care for the centurion of Capernaum (Matt. 8:1–12) and on that day said openly that the kingdom of God would be populated by those *outside*. After he saw the centurion's faith, he commented: "I say to you that many will come from the east and the west, and will take their places at the feast with Abraham, Isaac and Jacob in the kingdom of heaven. But the subjects of the kingdom will be thrown outside, into the darkness, where there will be weeping and gnashing of teeth" (8:11–12). These are Gentiles taking their place among God's own people.

Once Jesus entered the Gentile region of Gadara (east of Galilee) and there exorcised a Gentile man (Matt. 8:28–34). For some scholars, the feeding of the four thousand (15:32–39) is a miracle worked among non-Jews.[29]

THE FOOTHILLS LEADING TO MT. MERON IN UPPER GALILEE.

This is significant for our story because when Jesus travels north into Syria-Phoenicia, he will meet a Gentile woman. What he says to her is shocking, to say the least.

THE ENCOUNTER

On many occasions, Jesus retreated to the desolate hills of upper Galilee. Mark reports, "Very early in the morning, while it was still dark, Jesus got up, left the house and went off to a solitary place, where he prayed" (Mark 1:35). When things were stressful, he frequently departed by boat (Matt. 14:13). But it was the barrenness of the mountains northwest of the Sea of Galilee that he entered for refuge. He may have wandered near the ancient village of Sepph noted by the historian Josephus (*Jewish War* 2.573). Even today the remoteness of these regions has inspired many. Sepph may be the site of modern-day Safed, the home of Kabbalah (or Jewish mysticism).

It was less than twenty miles from Capernaum to the Roman province of Syria-Phoenicia beyond the northern mountains. Despite Jesus' absence in this area, his fame still was established here. Matthew writes, "News about him spread all over Syria, and people brought to him all who were ill with various diseases, those suffering severe pain, the demon-possessed, those having seizures, and the paralyzed; and he healed them"

A VIEW OF THE REMOTE, ISOLATED
HILLS OF UPPER GALILEE.

(Matt. 4:24). This must mean that Gentiles knew about him and had heard that he was able to do powerful things in God's name.

On one occasion Jesus departed for the northwest and entered "the region of Tyre and Sidon" (Matt. 15:21). I imagine

TYRE WAS A GREEK
CITY AND HAD MANY
STATUES SUCH AS THE
GREEK GOD ZEUS.

him looking for solitude, away from the villages and crowds. Matthew is careful with his words. Jesus did not enter Tyre; he entered its district. Mark adds that "he entered a house and did not want anyone to know it; yet he could not keep his presence secret" (Mark 7:24).

When Jesus arrives, a Gentile woman comes to him. The story also describes her carefully. She is Canaanite (like Rahab or Tamar, Matt. 1:3, 5) and "from that vicinity" (15:22). "Canaanite" is an old term used in the Old Testament (Heb. *kena'an*) to refer to coastal people who lived along the northern coasts. Mark uses different language to say the same thing: this woman is Greek, born in the province of Syria-Phoenicia (Mark 7:26).

Library of Congress, LC-USZC2-2473

ARTWORK BY CURRIER & IVES FROM THE NINTEENTH-CENTURY PORTRAYS JESUS AS A SHEPHERD LOOKING FOR HIS LOST SHEEP.

The woman sees Jesus and cries out, "Lord, Son of David, have mercy on me! My daughter is demon-possessed and suffering terribly" (Matt. 15:22). These are striking words coming from a Gentile. They echo precisely what Jews said earlier (9:27), and they will be heard again soon by other Jews (20:30). They are words of respect ("Lord"), and they betray that the woman understands something about Judaism. She uses a well-known Jewish title for the Messiah ("Son of David"), and by coming to him, she expresses her explicit faith in his charity.

Jesus' silence is also striking. Rather than heal the woman's daughter immediately, he ignores her. But she persists, crying out all the more so that even Jesus' disciples begin to complain. Jesus then clarifies the nature of his mission: "I was sent only to the lost sheep of Israel" (Matt. 15:24). Here he is simply applying to himself the same rule he had given to the disciples in 10:5–6. The work of the Jewish Messiah was primarily for Judaism, and his assignment was to find Judaism's lost sheep. But the woman persists even more. She falls on her knees before him and utters the words of a desperate mother: "Lord, help me!" (15:25).

THE SHOCKING WORD

Jesus' next words are some of the most famous in the Gospels. He echoes a proverb and seems to set a firm boundary between himself and the woman: "It is not right to take the children's bread and toss it to the dogs" (Matt. 15:26).

SECOND-CENTURY
ROMAN CARVING OF TWO
DOMESTIC DOGS.

Few sayings of Jesus have led more writers to express their disapproval. "Outrageous" and "arrogant" are a couple of the milder sentiments.[30] Is Jesus being rude to the woman to test her faith? Is this a little drama calling up old memories of Tyre and Israel—memories that were strained in the least?[31] Is there some cultural code behind this discussion that we miss entirely?

Even though the domestication of dogs happened quite early in human history, in first-century Judaism dogs were scavengers. Many roamed in packs outside villages (Psalm 59:6) looking for food. They were known for eating garbage and dung, and like vultures they devoured unburied corpses.[32] But they were never pets. Jews compared them with pigs and linked them with unclean animals (Isa. 66:3; 2 Peter 2:22).

The same is true throughout the Middle East today. Where Western culture has not changed Jewish attitudes, dogs live outside; they can be ferocious and at best serve as alarms for intruders. When the Israeli army laid siege to South Lebanon in 1982, the first thing they did in attacking an Arab village was to shoot all the dogs. To that army they were disposable.[33] For Westerners with a marked affection for dogs *as pets*, we can barely understand this.

Because of these cultural instincts, dogs were referred to with contempt in antiquity and became an easy metaphor for things despised. Even Jesus uses this cultural metaphor in his teaching (Matt. 7:6, "Do not give dogs what is sacred"). Among Jews it is easy to see how contempt for Gentiles picked up the metaphor. In Jewish speech, Gentiles were *dogs*.[34]

Therefore Jesus has set the boundary, and we are hard pressed to understand his meaning. It is true that the Greek term here denotes *little dogs* (Gk. *kyôn* is "dog"; *kynarion* is "little dog"), and while for us it may seem milder or perhaps cute, still, in first-century culture the edge remains. A dog is unclean, and in a Jewish sentence its use reflects a harsh statement.

Three things come immediately to mind. First, the problem with quoted speeches in the Gospels is that they lack any reference to tone.[35] We all know how meaning can be affected by the smallest change in the inflexion of the voice. (Imagine asking a child to do something and the many ways he or she might say, "Sure, Mom.") Meaning is conveyed by more than words, and without tone, words alone are sterile.

Second, we often forget that Jesus lived in a world that used proverbial sayings that *packaged* meaning, and it is only the literalist that might take them at face value. The proverbial saying will convey a history of conversation about a topic and its words are highly symbolic. The Middle East is filled with these. (Imagine saying to a person who is shading the truth, "Your nose is growing." The entire Pinocchio story lives behind this one phrase.)

Finally, posing the provocative or challenging question was a standard form of rabbinic teaching.[36] Rabbis would use irony frequently — just as Jesus does ("It is easier for a camel to go through the eye of a needle... "). In John 6:5 – 6 this is precisely how the feeding of the five thousand begins. Teaching was almost "Socratic," in which posed problems that seemed irresolvable are presented by the teacher to test students.

Therefore, reading Jesus here in cold print, failing to think about speech patterns and inflexion or even about Jesus' teaching tactics, may lead us astray. Something inspires the woman to reply with wit and humor. Does Jesus use a tone or smile that invites her to engage him? We do not know. At least we know this: Jesus did not practice prejudice against Gentiles. The balance of his ministry demonstrates it. But we also know that Jesus was laying down a priority. His messianic work belongs *first* to the Jews; efforts with Gentiles will come later. In Mark's version of the same saying, one small word makes this clear: "*First* let the children eat all they want ... for it is not right to take the children's bread and toss it to the dogs" (Mark 7:27). The children come first, but then the Gentiles will follow (see Paul's view in Rom. 1:16).

Somehow here Jesus does something that gives the woman an invitation to respond. The disciples want him to dismiss her, but Jesus refuses. Many Jewish teachers would have first tried to make her a convert; Jesus does not. Jesus merely speaks, and the woman intuits through what he says that his posture is open, receptive.

THE CLEVER RESPONSE

The woman is not unlike that character in Jesus' parable of the corrupt judge (Luke 18:1–8). Despite the resistance imposed on her, she pressed on until she gained what she needed. This woman near Tyre is no different. She understands the boundaries between herself and Jesus: they are little different than the boundaries between him and the Samaritan woman. And like that Samaritan woman, she has publicly acknowledged Jesus' authority ("Son of David," "Lord") before the disciples, who prefer her to go away. This is a woman who boldly persists. A Gentile could hardly expect privileges from a Jewish teacher. And yet because she knows Jesus is able to heal, she is willing to throw herself before him and beg for his help.

Greeks (unlike Jews) could have small pet dogs inside their homes. This woman takes advantage of the notion of a "dog" by spinning it in her own direction. The woman then pulls up

Christ and the Canaanite Woman, Drouais, Jean-Germain/Louvre, Paris, France/Giraudon/The Bridgeman Art Library

ARTWORK BY JEAN-GERMAIN DROUAIS (1763–1788) SHOWS THE WOMAN'S PERSISTENCE.

JESUS FED THE 4000 ON THE EAST SIDE OF THE SEA OF GALILEE NEAR HELLENISTIC CITIES SUCH AS HIPPOS.

her own proverbial saying no less clever than that of Jesus. She agrees with him—yes, the food of the children should not go to dogs—yes, the Jewish Messiah belongs to Judaism. And yet, "even the dogs eat the crumbs that fall from their master's table" (Matt. 15:27). Mark records it differently: "'Lord,' she replied, 'even the dogs under the table eat the children's crumbs'" (Mark 7:28). In one stroke, she has acknowledged the truth of Jesus' word, and at the same time she has brilliantly suggested that there still will be room for her. In an episode of verbal sparring, she holds her own.

Jesus is delighted. "Woman, you have great faith! Your request is granted" (Matt. 15:28). If tone or inflexion needs to be supplied, I can imagine Jesus smiling with amusement when he says this. This is the only time in all of Matthew's gospel where faith is described as "great." And curiously it is another Gentile, the Capernaum centurion, whose faith was also extolled so publicly by Jesus. In this woman Jesus witnesses a boldness and resilience that refuses to take no for an answer. She understands the limitations of her cultural place—but she presses beyond them and refuses to remain where she is.

When Matthew recorded this story, he was no doubt fascinated by what comes next. From Syria-Phoenicia, Jesus returns to the Sea of Galilee and immediately finds himself swarmed by the very crowds that required the earlier retreat (Matt. 15:29–31). His route takes him across the north side of the lake past Capernaum and Bethsaida and around to the east side (Mark tells us he comes to the "Decapolis," Mark 7:31). There, in a chiefly Gentile area, Jesus feeds four thousand men (along with their children and wives) with seven loaves of bread and a few fish. We also know he is on this eastern Gentile side because after the miracle, he boards a boat and crosses the lake to return to "Magadan," a likely reference to Magdala, on the western side.

The irony of this miracle is superb. *There is sufficient bread even for the Gentiles.* The woman of Tyre is correct. After giving her the "bread" she needs, Jesus continues in Gentile territory to distribute more "bread" than anyone knows he possesses. In each case, Jesus responds with compassion to the needs of his Gentile followers.

Faith and the Greek Woman of Tyre

This woman hidden away in one of the smallest stories of the Gospels is remarkable. She is a woman on a quest, a woman in whom perseverance, determination, and tenacity are working at full throttle. She cannot be dissuaded by cultural limits or by religious boundaries.

I am confident that gospel writers such as Matthew were careful to include little stories such as this because of their importance in forming faith among Christians who might read them later. The woman of Tyre has become a role model of what true faith might look like, and it has inspired so many.

Martin Luther's sixteenth-century sermon on this story is perhaps one of the most remarkable I have found. For Luther, this woman provides an example of "firm and perfect faith." Luther describes the apparent "closed door" that she experiences and writes:

> *All this does not lead her astray, neither does she take it to heart, but she continues immediately and firmly to cling in her confidence to the good news she had heard and embraced concerning him, and never*

MARTIN LUTHER, THE
GREAT FIFTEENTH-
CENTURY REFORMER.

gives up. We must also do the same and learn firmly to cling to the Word, even though God with all his creatures appears different than his Word teaches.

But, oh, how painful it is to nature and reason, that this woman should strip herself of self and forsake all that she experienced, and cling alone to God's bare Word, until she experienced the contrary.

May God help us in time of need and of death to possess like courage and faith![37]

NOTES

1. Matthew condenses the story in Matt. 9:18. Jairus declares in his initial contact that his daughter is dead. Mark has a longer narrative and (with Luke 8:40–56) has Jairus declare that the child is fatally ill, but she dies shortly thereafter. In the end all three Gospels record the same resurrection miracle, though Jairus's approach in Matthew is different.

2. Some scholars (such as A.-J. Levine) question whether menstrual impurity had social effects in the first century. She argues that Lev. 15 was not in effect but offers no evidence to that end. We also have other outlines of requirements from the period: Qumran (11QTemple 48:14 – 1 – 17) and the oral law (Mishnah tractate *Niddah*) suggest that interest in restrictions did not disappear. See also S. L. Love, "Jesus Heals the Hemorrhaging Woman," in *The Social Setting of Jesus and the Gospels* (ed. W. Stegemann, B. Malina, G. Theissen; Minneapolis: Fortress, 2002), 85–102.

3. H. L. Strack and P. Billerbeck, *Kommentar zum Neuen Testament aus Talmud und Midrasch* (1922), cited by W. Lane, *The Gospel of Mark* (Grand Rapids: Eerdmans, 1974), 196 n. 62.

4. See the apocryphal *Gospel of Nicodemus* (also known as the *Acts of Pilate*), chapter 7.

5. The Jewish historian Josephus gives a full description of Jericho in his account of the Jewish wars in the first century BC (see *Jewish War* 1.21.9).

6. Following the destruction of the temple in AD 70, Rome replaced this tax with its own tax as repayment for the war (the *fiscus judaicus* tax). See Josephus, *Jewish War* 7.218.

7. Josephus, *Antiquities* 17.318.

8. Josephus, *Jewish War* 2.403, 405.

9. K. C. Hanson, "The Galilean Fishing Economy and the Jesus Tradition," *Biblical Theology Bulletin* 27 (1997): 99–111.

10. Daniel B. Wallace, *Greek Grammar beyond the Basics: An Exegetical Syntax of the New Testament* (Grand Rapids: Zondervan, 1996), 536.

11. Joel Green, *The Gospel of Luke* (New International Commentary on the New Testament; Grand Rapids: Eerdmans, 1997), 672.

12. Richard Horsley, *Archaeology, History and Society in Galilee* (Harrisburg, PA: Trinity Press International, 1996), 112–18.

13. There are Roman baths in east Capernaum at the Greek Orthodox sector (an area rarely visited), but their date is uncertain.

14. See J. L. Reed, *Archaeology and the Galilean Jesus: A Reexamination of the Evidence* (Harrisburg, PA: Trinity Press International, 2002), and James H. Charlesworth, *Jesus and Archaeology* (Grand Rapids: Eerdmans, 2006).

15. *De re militari* 2.14.

16. This leads to the suggestion that east of Capernaum (the Orthodox compound) may contain Roman ruins that come from this period.

17. Oddly, a *mikveh* has not been located in Capernaum even though it was a Jewish town. Perhaps the lake was used as the site for ritual washing.

18. *The Gallic Wars* 2.33.

19. See Bruce Winter, *Seek the Welfare of the City* (Grand Rapids: Eerdmans, 1994), 26–30.

20. R. France, *The Gospel of Matthew* (Grand Rapids: Eerdmans, 2007), 316–19.

21. However, the Jewish historian Josephus tells us that Galileans did travel through Samaria en route to Jerusalem for the annual feasts (*Antiquities* 20:118). But Josephus does not give convincing evidence that the Samaritan route was commonplace for religiously conservative Jews.

22. Josephus, *Antiquities* 18.29–30; cf. A. D. Crown, *The Samaritans* (Tübingen: J. C. B. Mohr, 1989), 21.

23. John likely has a literary interest in betrothal scenes. In John 20, Mary meets the resurrected Jesus alone in a garden surrounded by spices. This is a scene reminiscent of the Song of Songs.

24. R. Bull, "An Archeological Context for Understanding John 4," *Biblical Archeologist* 38 (1975): 54–59.

25. Mishnah, *Mikva'oth* 1:1–8.

26. Arrian of Nicomedia, *History of Alexander* 2:18–24.

27. We know a great deal about Judea's relationship with Tyre. See G. Theissen, *The Gospels in Context: The Social and Political History in the Synoptic Tradition* (Minneapolis: Fortress, 1991), 65–80.

28. This is a tremendous subject of controversy among scholars. See recently M. Bird, *Jesus and the Origins of the Gentile Mission* (New York: T&T Clark, 2006).

29. R. T. France, *The Gospel of Matthew* (Grand Rapids: Eerdmans, 2007), 591.

30. Feminist and postcolonial interpretations of the passage are severe. See particularly M. W. Dube, *Postcolonial Feminist Interpretation of the Bible* (St. Louis: Chalice, 2000), 157–95.

31. J. D. M. Darrett, "Law in the New Testament: The Syro-Phoenician Woman and the Centurion of Capernaum," *Novum Testamentum* 15.3 (1973):161–86.

32. For copious references from classical literature, see Craig Keener, *A Commentary on the Gospel of Matthew* (Grand Rapids: Eerdmans, 1999), 416–17.

33. This theme of killing dogs in the Israeli occupation of Lebanon from 1982–2000 became a symbolic motif in the Israeli animated film by Ari Folman, *Waltz with Bashir* (2008).

34. See Darrett, "Law in the New Testament," 147 n. 3.

35. This has been underscored by G. B. Caird, *Theology of the New Testament* (Oxford: Clarendon, 1994), 395; on voice inflexion, see his *Language and Imagery in the Bible* (London: Duckworth, 1980), 53–55.

36. D. Daube, *The New Testament and Rabbinic Judaism* (London: Athlone, 1956), 158–69.

37. Martin Luther, *The Sermons of Martin Luther* (trans. J. N. Lenker; Grand Rapids: Baker, reprint 2000), 2:148–54. This resource was identified by a young theologian, Matthew Draft.

Share Your Thoughts

With the Author: Your comments will be forwarded to the author when you send them to *zauthor@zondervan.com*.

With Zondervan: Submit your review of this book by writing to *zreview@zondervan.com*.

Free Online Resources at
www.zondervan.com

Zondervan AuthorTracker: Be notified whenever your favorite authors publish new books, go on tour, or post an update about what's happening in their lives at www.zondervan.com/authortracker.

Daily Bible Verses and Devotions: Enrich your life with daily Bible verses or devotions that help you start every morning focused on God. Visit www.zondervan.com/newsletters.

Free Email Publications: Sign up for newsletters on Christian living, academic resources, church ministry, fiction, children's resources, and more. Visit www.zondervan.com/newsletters.

Zondervan Bible Search: Find and compare Bible passages in a variety of translations at www.zondervanbiblesearch.com.

Other Benefits: Register yourself to receive online benefits like coupons and special offers, or to participate in research.

ZONDERVAN®

ZONDERVAN.com/
AUTHORTRACKER
follow your favorite authors